The Next Conversation Workbook

Also by Jefferson Fisher

The Next Conversation

The Next Conversation Workbook

Practical Exercises for
Arguing Less and Talking More

Jefferson Fisher

PENGUIN LIFE

AN IMPRINT OF

PENGUIN BOOKS

PENGUIN LIFE

UK | USA | Canada | Ireland | Australia
India | New Zealand | South Africa

Penguin Life is part of the Penguin Random House group of companies whose addresses can be found at global.penguinrandomhouse.com.

Penguin Random House UK,
One Embassy Gardens, 8 Viaduct Gardens, London SW11 7BW

penguin.co.uk

First published in the United States of America by Tarcher, an imprint of Penguin Random House LLC, 2026
First published in Great Britain by Penguin Life 2026
001

Copyright © Jefferson Fisher, 2026

The moral right of the author has been asserted

Penguin Random House values and supports copyright. Copyright fuels creativity, encourages diverse voices, promotes freedom of expression and supports a vibrant culture. Thank you for purchasing an authorized edition of this book and for respecting intellectual property laws by not reproducing, scanning or distributing any part of it by any means without permission. You are supporting authors and enabling Penguin Random House to continue to publish books for everyone. No part of this book may be used or reproduced in any manner for the purpose of training artificial intelligence technologies or systems. In accordance with Article 4(3) of the DSM Directive 2019/790, Penguin Random House expressly reserves this work from the text and data mining exception

Printed and bound in Italy by L.E.G.O. S.p.A

The authorized representative in the EEA is Penguin Random House Ireland, Morrison Chambers, 32 Nassau Street, Dublin D02 YH68

A CIP catalogue record for this book is available from the British Library

ISBN: 978–0–241–80572–5

Penguin Random House is committed to a sustainable future for our business, our readers and our planet. This book is made from Forest Stewardship Council® certified paper.

Contents

Introduction • ix

Part I
The Essentials • 1

Part II
The Application • 17

RULE 1
Say It with Control • 19

Control Yourself • 21
Control the Moment • 37
Control the Pace • 51

RULE 2
Say It with Confidence • 63

Assertive Voice • 67
Difficult People • 87
Boundaries • 105

RULE 3
Say It to Connect • 123

Frames • 125
Defensiveness • 135
Difficult Conversations • 149

Answer Key • 167
Your Next Steps • 173

INTRODUCTION

Kelly had spent her whole life chasing her mother's approval. Perfect grades, the right kind of boyfriends, even sacrificing her own desires. None of it ever earned her mother's acknowledgment. Then one day during an argument, her mother pulled out the same old line that Kelly had heard for forty years: "Well, I'm sorry I'm such a horrible mother."

In the past, that guilt trip would have worked. Kelly would have spent the next thirty minutes reassuring her mother, listing all the ways she was grateful for her sacrifices. But Kelly had recently come across my videos on handling bad apologies. So this time was different. This time, Kelly didn't take the bait.

Instead, she took a breath, met her mother's eyes, and said, "I'm willing to accept an apology."

In that moment, something shifted. For the first time, Kelly realized she didn't need her mother's approval. She only needed her own voice.

Daniel was always the good guy. Still is. But for years he'd prioritized keeping the peace over speaking his mind, even when he strongly disagreed. In board meetings, he stayed quiet. In one-on-one conversations, he held back. Then came the moment that changed everything.

During his annual project presentation to the executive team, a senior manager dismissed a key part of his plan as a failure. Normally, Daniel would have swallowed the criticism, nodded along, and let it go—anything to avoid conflict. But this time was different. He'd recently seen my videos on Instagram.

With a steady voice, he said, "I see things differently."

The room went silent. All eyes turned to him. Daniel took his time and confidently walked the team through the logic and strategy behind his plan. When he finished, the energy in the room had shifted. He hadn't just defended his work—he had commanded the room. The board approved his plan, not only because of the strategy but because of the way his words stood behind it.

Hanna had spent years overexplaining—why she couldn't make it to girls' night, why she didn't eat certain foods, why she needed time alone. She believed that if she just said enough things, if she gave the right reasons, people would understand. More words meant more credibility. More acceptance. Less disappointment. But one day, something changed.

When invited to an event she didn't want to attend, Hanna recalled my advice and simply said, "I can't. Thank you for the invitation." When the person pressed for a reason, she didn't fall into old habits. Instead, she calmly replied, "I can't make it. I'm sure it'll be a great time."

No justifications. No explanations. No guilt.

And to her surprise—the world didn't crumble.

Like these people, you know that same truth: the problem isn't *what* to say; it's *how* to say it.

Deep down, you already know what you want to say to your friend or boss or spouse. That conversation you know you need to have but you've been putting off because you know it'll be hard. You have the words. You have the pieces. You just need the steps.

INTRODUCTION

That's what *The Next Conversation* framework offers: a simple, proven communication method to build better relationships and, more importantly, a better you.

By the time you finish this workbook, you will be able to:

- Control your communication (even in the most difficult conversation)

- Find—and use—your assertive voice

- Stand up for yourself

- Communicate and enforce your boundaries

- Overcome others' defensiveness (and prevent your own)

You will learn how to speak boldly, with your chin up, and to embrace the vulnerability that comes with laying all your cards on the table.

As I told you in *The Next Conversation*, I'm not an academic researcher, therapist, or psychologist. I'm a trial attorney from a long line of lawyers who had one characteristic in common: knowing the art of communication. In the following pages, I want to share the lessons I've learned over a lifetime of arguments, disagreements, heated debates, and difficult conversations. I know they'll work for you because I've seen them work—not only for me but also for the millions of people who've implemented my techniques from my social media videos.

How to Use This Book

You don't need to have read *The Next Conversation* to use this workbook. For each section and tactic, I provide a brief summary of the relevant points, sometimes even using words from *The Next Conversation*. If you want to dig deeper into any aspect, I provide page numbers for where to find the information in the original book. This workbook is yours to tear up, break down, and use however it works best for you. Here's a quick rundown that will help you get the most out of this workbook:

1. **Go in order (ideally).** As tempting as it might be, don't skip to what seems most interesting or what you most need help with right now. Each main step builds upon the former step, and I often reference certain strategies multiple times.

2. **Go slow.** Don't rush yourself. Don't make this another item on your to-do list. Many of the questions will ask you to consider the stuff of life: your relationships, your conversations, your feelings. Don't fill in the blanks just to have the blanks filled in. Give yourself the undistracted time to think through your answers.

3. **Start small.** Don't overwhelm yourself. There is a lot of information here. Use one takeaway at a time until it becomes more natural for you, then add another. For some people, using these strategies will be a big shift in how they relate to others. Give yourself time to acclimate to your new normal before using more strategies.

4. **Start today.** As soon as you read a strategy, look for opportunities to use it in your everyday life. In your next text. Your next email. Even if it's addressing a relatively small, mundane issue, it could be the perfect time for you to practice something new. The more you practice, the more comfortable you'll become using these ideas. And the more ready you'll be when the true tests come.

5. **Seek accountability.** With the right person, accountability motivates change. Let your partner, close friend, or family member know that you're working to become a better, more confident

communicator. Ask them to routinely ask you, "What have you learned this week?" and "How have you used that this week?" This is exactly what we do within my School of Communication online membership community to support one another.

6. **Optional: keep a running journal.** While there's space at the end of each part to journal your thoughts about that topic, you may want to consider keeping a separate journal to record how these strategies go when you use them throughout your day. Ask yourself questions like:

   - "What progress have I seen in myself?"
   - "How are others responding to me?"
   - "What's making me uncomfortable?"

Journaling is a great way to witness your progress over time. If you're not a fan of one-to-one accountability, let your journal be your accountability partner.

About the Exercises

Most of the exercises are open-ended questions, but you'll also be asked to grade yourself, to choose items from a checklist, to fill in blanks, and to create and resolve scenarios.

For every exercise, the goal is for you to think more deeply about how you currently have conversations and how you *could* have conversations—the kind that make you feel good about yourself, even when the topic is hard.

As a basic guideline, give yourself thirty minutes to an hour to work through each section. The biggest thing is not to rush.

Are you ready?

Take a breath and turn the page. We've got work to do.

The Next Conversation Workbook

Part I

The Essentials

Over the next few pages, we're going to work through the essentials of my framework. The essentials focus on connecting with yourself before you connect with others. I want you to understand these foundational principles so that the tools and techniques I offer have their best chance of making the most difference in your conversations, your relationships, and your life.

First, let's set a destination. You picked up this workbook for a reason. Let's get specific about why.

What Are Your Goals?

Review the following issues that my followers have told me they struggle with. Check the boxes that you could have written or that you've thought about at some point.

- ☐ Being assertive without being confrontational

- ☐ Focusing on what the other person is saying without thinking about what to say next

- ☐ Setting boundaries or expectations when I haven't established them early on

- ☐ Stopping myself from protecting other people's feelings

- ☐ Keeping emotions out of hot topics, like politics or religion

- ☐ Tactfully handling sarcasm or condescending remarks

- ☐ Communicating with someone who ignores my statements, turns the conversation to talking about themselves, or one-ups me

- ☐ Overcoming a conversation going in circles

- ☐ Knowing what to say when I need to say it most

What other communication issues do you struggle with?

_____

_____

_____

_____

For each issue listed that affects your life, transform it into a goal. Make it specific, realistic, and actionable.

For example, if you checked "Keeping emotions out of hot topics," your goal could be, "I will remind myself to take a deep breath before responding when other people bring up troubling topics." (Note: we'll get much more into breathing soon.)

THE ESSENTIALS

Also, if you're not sure what your goals are right now, that's cool too. Don't get stuck here. With dozens of examples throughout this workbook, your specific goals will become clear as you go. If a new goal comes to mind, come back to this section and add it to your list.

I will _____.

I will _____.

I will _____.

I will _____.

I will _____.

Now I want you to imagine yourself a year from now. You've met all of your goals and routinely use them in your conversations and relationships. What do you fear will happen in your relationships if that holds true? It may help to think of a specific person (maybe your most difficult relationship) and ask yourself, "If I speak and act in this new way with this person, how do I fear they might respond?"

_____

_____

_____

_____

Lastly, once you meet these goals, how will your life and relationships change for the better? Put another way, what do you want to accomplish by the time you've completed this workbook?

_____

_____

_____

Now that you have a clearer understanding of where you want to go, here's how you can get there. The page numbers in parentheses are where you can find the information in *The Next Conversation* if you want to go more in-depth on a concept.

Never Win an Argument (*TNC*, pp. 21–39)

Arguments aren't something to win. They're something to unravel.

Think of arguments like knots in a conversation. If you pull in your direction and your friend pulls in theirs, what happens? The knot tightens. It becomes harder and harder to undo. If you both dig in your heels, then you're stuck in a game of tug-of-war.

So drop the rope. Stop trying to win.

Instead, see the knot as an opportunity for connection. That means rather than yelling right back at them, you take a mindset that asks yourself, "Where is their behavior coming from?" Start at the loose ends by getting curious about the other person until you understand the heart of the matter. You can even ask the other person, "How can we smooth this knot out together?" or say, "Help me find the knot."

Real communication begins when you get past their struggles, fears, and hopes. Real communication begins when you discover their why.

Asking yourself questions like "Who am I really talking to?" and "What else

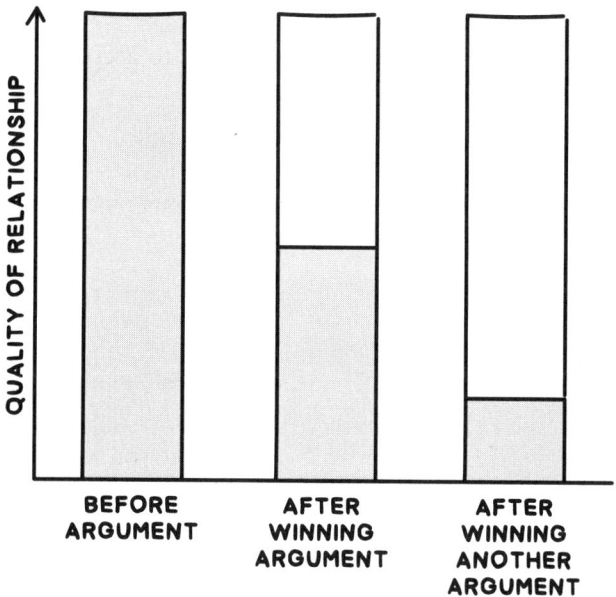

is at play?" opens doors to connection. Remember: the person you see isn't the person you're talking to. Like you, their life is still going on in the background of their conversation. Think of a river and its undercurrent. There's so much more going on under the surface that you can't see.

Instead of making arguments about the moment, I'm going to teach you how to turn arguments into conversations about discovering that person. It doesn't take much to dive beneath a person's struggle—but it does take a willingness to give up the fight. Real communication begins when you can discern the struggle, the fear, or the hope hiding underneath.

Fun fact: *The Next Conversation* was almost titled *The Confidence to Connect*. Nowhere is this confidence more necessary than in hard conversations and yelling matches. In the moment when your fight-or-flight response wants nothing to do with the other person, choosing to connect is an act of mind-body defiance. You're pressing pause on your predisposed response to act on the more intentional, more thoughtful way to relate to the person across from you.

That's real communication.

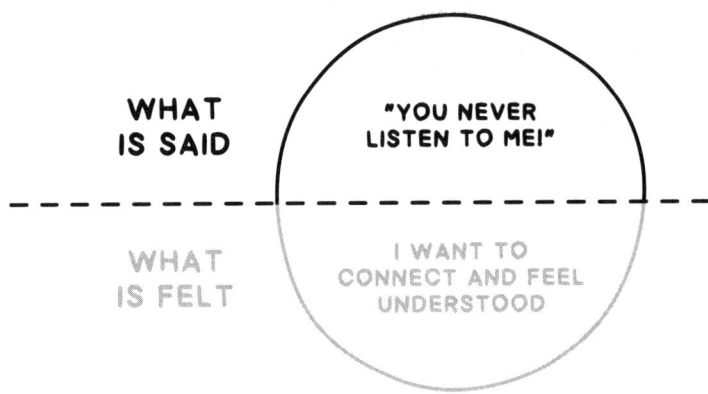

How often do you feel the need to win arguments?

_____

_____

What drives your need to win arguments?

_____

_____

What do you fear will happen if you don't "win"?

_____

_____

Based on what you read in this section, how might you need to change your approach to arguments?

_____

_____

_____

_____

_____

Your Next Conversation (*TNC*, pp. 41–54)

How often does a rehearsed conversation in your head turn out the way you imagined in real life?

Next to never. You're more likely to get me to eat a pickle. And I hate pickles.

There are better ways to spend your time before your next conversation: set a goal and set your values. Conversational goals and values make sure that you know where you want to go in the conversation, like true north on a compass.

The next time you're facing a difficult conversation, set a goal *before* it starts. Don't wait until you're talking in the middle of a heated conversation to figure out what you want to say.

Make the goal realistic and reachable. For example, rather than going in expecting the other person to issue you an immediate apology (highly unlikely), try going in with the goal that you want them to know you care for them (more likely). At its most basic level, your goals for every conversation should align with this mindset:

Have something to learn, not something to prove.

WHEN YOUR CONVERSATION HAS GOALS

What unrealistic goals have you had in past conversations? For example, believing one conversation will cure all other underlying relationship problems.

_____

_____

_____

For each unrealistic goal listed, what would have been a more achievable goal? For example, agreeing on steps to mitigate or eliminate the recurrence of the issue.

_____

_____

_____

To set better goals for your next conversation, prepare yourself by asking questions like:

- If I had to choose, what's the one thing that I need them to understand?

- What small step can I take to show them that I heard them?

- What assumptions am I making?

- How can I show gratitude for this opportunity to talk?

- Is there a part of this that I'm trying to win?

Next, set values for your conversation.

Your conversational values answer the question "How will I show up for myself?" For example, if you value honesty, you'll choose to tell the truth instead of sugarcoating. You'll stop pretending things are okay when they're not and start giving yourself permission to speak up.

Conversational values are often aspirational, meaning that they're what you want to see happen in your life. Some people immediately know their answers. If you struggle to name your values, here's a helpful exercise: list the values you admire in your friends below.

_____

_____

_____

_____

_____

_____

To take it a brave step further, ask your friends or loved ones these questions about yourself.

- What do you think I find important in my life based on our daily conversations?
- What are three words you would use to describe my character to someone who doesn't know me?
- What topics of conversation do I get most enthusiastic about?
- What quality is most important to me in the friendships I have?
- What emotion do you wish I'd show more of?

When you receive replies, reflect. What responses surprised you and why?

_____

_____

_____

_____

Which ones confirmed what you knew or felt?

_____

_____

_____

How do any of the answers change what you think about yourself? Or how you want to change yourself?

_____

_____

_____

_____

Based on your own sense of self, the responses you received, and the change you want to experience, write down your three deepest conversational values. These can be a single word, a phrase, or a full sentence. For example, one of mine is "If I can't be a bridge, I'll be a lighthouse."

1. _____

2. _____

3. _____

When you align your conversation with your values, you're prepared to meet your goal *before* the conversation even starts.

You can change *everything* in your next conversation.

But only if you're willing to change your mindset first.

The Truth About Connection (*TNC*, pp. 55–65)

Time stands still as you text your friend and see their typing indicator in reply.

> Can we talk about what I said the other day?

> . . .

The ellipsis suddenly disappears and no other message arrives.

If you're not careful, your mind can start to race. *What were they going to type? Are they too busy for me?* Your assumptions may even go off the deep end. *Did I say something wrong? Are they mad at me? Should I wait or text again?*

Now let's change the setting.

You bump into your friend at your favorite coffee shop. You briefly catch up, then you ask, "Can we talk about what I said the other day?"

They hesitate. They look down. You hear a quiet sigh.

You reply, "That's okay. I can see now isn't a good time. Let's talk later?"

They nod and say, "I'd like that." Seeing their face and willingness, you immediately feel more assured and better—no mind racing, no second thoughts.

That's the difference between transmission and connection in communication.

Transmission focuses on sending and receiving signals over a distance. It's transactional. It's about conveying data. You experience transmission in texts, emails, or online messaging.

Connection, on the other hand, has warmth. It's human. It's sharing information with depth and emotional nuance. You experience connection when you speak face-to-face, and it touches your deepest needs for belonging, understanding, and expression.

I'm *absolutely* not saying you shouldn't text or email anyone—transmission is essential to our everyday life. In fact, with some people (think aggressive or toxic), texting or emailing is the safer option. But problems come when you start to believe transmission is an all-out replacement for connection. It's not.

You're meant to feel the warmth of seeing someone's smile, not read it in an emoji.

Connection has two components: understanding and acknowledgment. And you need both. For example, if I understand you but you can't tell, you won't connect with me. And if I acknowledge what you're saying but I still don't understand it, I won't connect with you.

THE ESSENTIALS

Remember, you can't choose the outcome in your next conversation. You can only choose whether or not to try to connect.

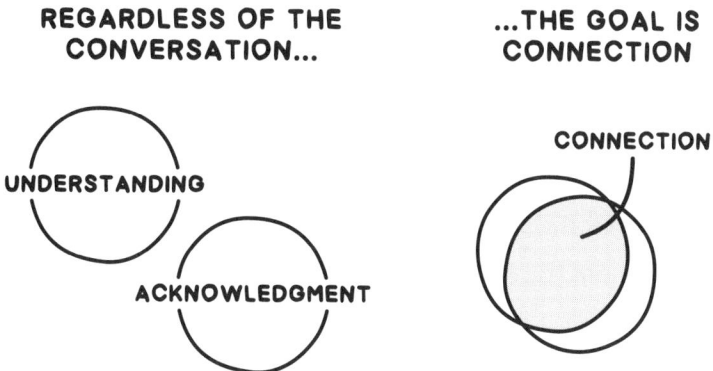

We tend to cut off connection with others in three ways:

- **Lack of awareness:** Ever had someone say "You look mad" or ask "What's wrong?" when you feel perfectly happy and content? When you're talking, you may not realize that your eyebrows are scrunched or your tone is harsher than you intended. Maybe you know someone (not you, of course) with a "resting" face that looks mad when they're not smiling. Without self-awareness, you're often unaware of the mixed signals you send.

- **Lack of understanding:** Have you heard someone begin by saying "I just don't understand how they can . . ."? Whenever I hear that, I always think to myself, *Well, have you tried?* Most of the time, conflict occurs because you've decided to argue against their *point* rather than acknowledge and address their *perspective*. When you fail to appreciate the difference in someone's perspective versus your own, you will always have a hard time understanding what they're saying and why they're saying it.

- **Lack of self-assurance:** There are everyday verbal and visual cues that tell others about your level of assurance behind your words. Maybe it's insecure body language, hedging words, or doubting phrases (like adding "Does that make sense?"). If you don't feel assured about what you're saying, the other person won't feel sure to believe it, follow it, or accept it. When you lack self-assurance in communication, you will begin to hide from the very interactions that could bring out the best of you.

Each of these barriers to connection can be removed, and the strategies you'll work through in part two will help you accomplish that.

Do you prefer transmission (texting or emailing) or connection (phone calls or in-person visits)?

_____

Why is that the case?

_____

_____

What would need to happen for you to seek more connection in your life?

_____

THE ESSENTIALS

Which of the three barriers to communication listed do you struggle with most and why?

_____

_____

And just like that, you've learned the essentials to put *The Next Conversation* framework to work for you. Take some time to let these ideas sink in. In part two, we're going to build upon this foundation.

It's about to get practical, y'all.

Part II

The Application

The Next Conversation framework is simple.

1. Say it with control.
2. Say it with confidence.
3. Say it to connect.

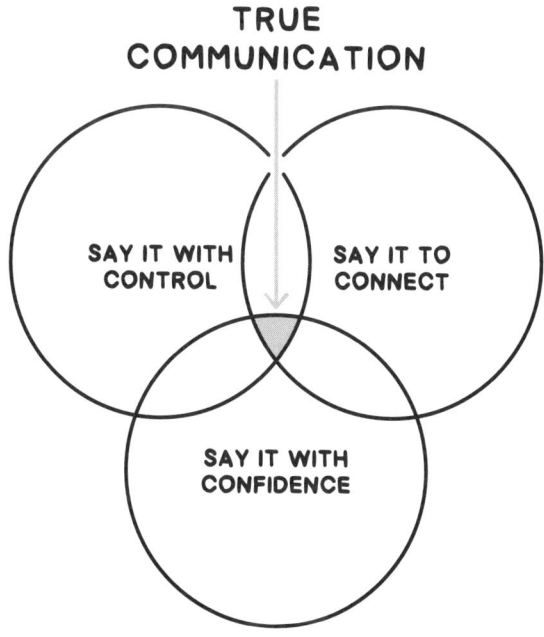

But each step has specific strategies that have proven effective for me, my clients, and my followers. I encourage you to work through these sections sequentially and not to bite off more than you can chew.

When a strategy sticks out as something you know will make you a better communicator, use it in your next conversation. See how it feels. See what happens. The more you practice these steps, the more they'll become second nature—and the more confident you'll be.

RULE 1

Say It with Control

Once, I had a trial involving a big commercial dispute. On day four, the courtroom turned tense. I was cross-examining the opposing party's corporate representative and his testimony was pivotal. When the tension was heaviest, I offered a piece of evidence as an exhibit into the record: an internal email from the other company that would undermine their entire defense. Immediately, the other side's lawyer stood up. "Objection!" he cried, explaining why the evidence shouldn't be allowed. The court quickly overruled his objection and gave me the go-ahead to proceed with my questioning.

After the case was over, the attorneys had a chance to talk to the jury and get their feedback on the case. When it was my turn, I asked, "Did the internal email I brought into evidence sway any part of your decision?"

It was a unanimous "Nope."

"It wasn't your exhibit," the jury explained. "It was the other attorney." Apparently, after my opposing counsel had objected to the exhibit, he looked angry—for one fleeting moment—at the judge's ruling before sitting back down. And the jury saw. That flash of anger and disappointment told the jury that whatever testimony they were about to hear, the other attorney didn't want them to hear it. As if he were trying to hide something from them. Ultimately, it was the attorney's reaction that had the most sway in their verdict, finding for my client. Not the document itself.

Reacting emotionally is normal. I knew the opposing attorney well as a friend, and he certainly wasn't trying to hide anything. It was simply his reaction to losing the argument. He didn't even know he looked upset.

In the face of intense conversation, how can you control your emotions?

To speak your point of view, your needs, and your truth—to make yourself truly heard, seen, and understood—you need to learn control.

Just think about the leaders you admire. You listen to them because they speak with control. What if you could talk like them in any conversation, and especially in your most challenging conversations?

I know you can.

The best way to do this is to follow three simple guidelines:

1. Control yourself.
2. Control the moment.
3. Control the pace.

Once you learn this control, you'll experience a power beyond words. You may hear a voice coming from within that you've never heard before—the one that's always been ready to speak but has been silenced by fear or shame or neglect.

Your true voice.

The one that's measured, thoughtful, and ready to respond authentically to anyone about anything at any time.

But you have to master the wildest variable first: yourself.

Control Yourself

Chapter 4 in *The Next Conversation*

Think about the last time you lost control of yourself. Maybe you said something you instantly regretted. Or you acted aggressively toward someone and surprised yourself at how out of character it was. Or maybe you wanted to speak your mind but felt forced to remain quiet.

No matter what led to your loss of self-control, the results were likely the same: regret that you didn't handle the conversation better and a desire to approach the next conversation with higher intentions. If only you'd had self-control, you could've stopped yourself from saying what you shouldn't or encouraged yourself to say what you should.

Yet we often have the hardest time controlling ourselves in the moments we most need to, like in difficult conversations and arguments. In the very defining moments of our lives where we need to stand up for ourselves.

If we could exercise a few degrees more self-control in our relationships and our conversations, our connections would deepen. We would be better known, and we would better know others.

So let's discover where you're losing control—and how to take it back.

The Two Phases of Every Argument (*TNC*, pp. 74–80)

Every argument has an ignition phase and a cooling phase.

Ignition happens when, with enough friction, the productive becomes destructive. Something about the interaction rubs you the wrong way. You resented a word. You didn't appreciate the other person's tone. You didn't like their look. With limited time and enough friction, heat builds. And before you know it, you're on fire.

Ignition happens the moment you:

- Light a match (feel threatened)

- Blow a fuse (get defensive)

- Go nuclear (launch personal attacks)

Cooling occurs when the heat begins to dissipate. Cooling happens the moment you:

- Turn off the heat (walk away)

- Put out the fire (come to a mutual understanding)

- Or there's nothing left to burn (reach impasse)

Whichever route you took, the temperature stops rising and starts to come down. The smoke clears and the frustration lifts. Clarity enters the conversation. You regain awareness of the importance of the relationship and why (or if) the other person matters to you.

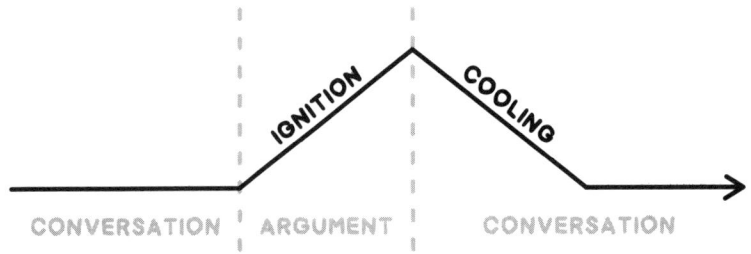

But it's hard to know all of that is going on while you're arguing. So let's dive deeper.

Check your temp

Pause here to allow yourself to get into a quiet, reflective mood.

Bring your last major argument to mind. Close your eyes and call up the scene as if it's a movie inside your head. You're no longer the star of the show. You're a spectator. Let the scene unfold before you. If it brings up difficult or uncomfortable feelings, take a few deep breaths to re-center yourself before continuing. The goal here is to be as objective as possible about what happened—an unbiased audience member recounting exactly what you saw on the screen.

With that moment in mind, answer the following questions.

What temperature did your argument begin at? Fill in the thermometer.

What words or phrases from either person turned up the temperature?

_____

_____

What nonverbal communication increased the heat?

- Body language, e.g., crossed arms
- Invading personal space
- Silence
- Facial expression

- Lack of eye contact
- Staring
- Other: _____

How high did the temperature get?

What did either person say to cool the argument?

_____

_____

What did you do to cool the argument?

- Softened tone
- Apologized
- Clarified
- Agreed
- Walked away
- Other: _____

What did they do to cool the argument?

- Softened tone
- Apologized
- Clarified
- Agreed
- Walked away
- Other: _____

When the argument ended, what was the final temperature?

In reviewing a past argument this way, what have you learned about yourself?

_____

_____

_____

_____

What do you wish you would have said or done differently?

___

___

___

___

How Your Body Controls Your Response (*TNC*, pp. 80–83)

To better control yourself during conflict, you have to know what's happening inside you.

Physiologically speaking, the ignition phase is your fight-or-flight response. You feel threatened and want to attack or escape. You want to say something hurtful or storm out of the room. This is your sympathetic nervous system automatically firing up to protect you from threats, even verbal ones.

Your body, unfortunately, typically has a slower reaction time than your emotions, often resulting in emotion-driven rather than logic-driven behavior (think yelling, crying, or the knee-jerk hurtful comment). That's why you're sometimes surprised at the severity of your response in a given situation or conversation. You think, *I shouldn't say that*, at the same moment you say an angry word. You've turned up the heat but still wonder who's at fault—as if there's another person inside you who just won't obey.

Now think about your typical response to a threat. The threat can be real or perceived, verbal or physical. On the spectrum below, draw an X where your response falls.

You can know your ignition phase is flaring when:

- ☐ You feel a prickling sensation.
- ☐ Your pupils become dilated.
- ☐ Your cheeks flush.
- ☐ Your breathing quickens and becomes shallow.
- ☐ Your heart rate elevates.
- ☐ Your muscles tense.
- ☐ Your hands shake.
- ☐ You think irrationally.
- ☐ Other: _____

Read that list again and check any sensation you've experienced when threatened. If you don't see your response, write it in.

Now let's consider the cooling phase, aka your rest-and-digest response. Rest wants to step back and take a breather. Digest seeks to recharge or balance the mood. This is your parasympathetic nervous system working to return your body to its natural state.

In this state, you can think clearly and rationally because your emotions aren't running the show. This is also when remorse or regret may show up for what you said or did in the heat of the argument. This phase allows you to better understand what you intended, what actually happened, and what you may have to do in your next conversation to mend the relationship.

When an argument cools, what's your typical response? Draw an X where you fall.

REST ⊢──────────────────────────────⊣ **DIGEST**

You can know your cooling phase is descending when:

- ☐ You feel drained, sad, or exhausted.
- ☐ Your nerves or "jitters" die down.
- ☐ Your vision widens.
- ☐ You tear up or cry.
- ☐ Your breathing returns to normal.
- ☐ Your heart rate slows.
- ☐ Your muscles relax.
- ☐ Rationality returns.
- ☐ Other: _____

Read that list again and check what you've experienced in a cooling phase.

Now think about the last time you had an argument that really got under your skin. (Feel free to use the same argument from the previous section.) How do you think the other person would describe your ignition phase? How would they describe your cooling phase? Consider what they saw and heard from you in both phases.

There's no escaping your ignition and cooling phases. We're all wired that way. So the choice isn't to prevent the friction that leads to ignition. Neither is it to immediately blame the other person. Rather, your decision is to see your internal response as a natural reaction that requires further curiosity and digging on your part. Realize that friction offers room for improvement.

Because what triggers you teaches you.

Meet Your Triggers (*TNC*, pp. 83–89)

We all have certain experiences (or people) that immediately trigger us. When confronted with one, you feel a strong, negative reaction. You just can't help yourself. And it can be downright impossible to act like a normal human being in that moment.

So how can you be proactive about your reactions?

Learn your triggers.

Triggers can be physical or psychological. Physical triggers are the most noticeable. If someone aggressively runs toward you, your body will instinctually react. But physical triggers don't play as large of a role in communication as your psychological triggers do. These triggers occur more frequently and more subtly.

Psychological triggers happen in three ways.

1. **Social evaluation triggers** involve the fear of negative judgment, rejection, or humiliation.

2. **Personal identity triggers** challenge your competence, autonomy, purpose, or values.

3. **Loss triggers** stem from the fear of losing someone or something you value, like a job or a certain status.

Let's see how these triggers may show up in your life. For each trigger that follows, complete the sentence or answer the question.

Your social evaluation triggers

These types of triggers concern how you believe others perceive you.

- If I say "I don't agree," I fear the other person will see me as an enemy.

- If I say no to a social invitation, I fear the other person will exclude me in the future.

- If I don't dress a certain way, I fear people will view me as an outcast.

Social evaluation triggers stem from caring deeply about what others think about you. Their recurring theme is vulnerability.

On a scale of 1 (yours) to 5 (theirs), whose opinion of you matters more to you?

On a scale of 1 (never) to 5 (always), how would you rate your tendency to people please?

What do you notice about the difference between your answers to the previous two questions? What might this tell you about your social evaluation triggers?

_____

_____

_____

_____

Your personal identity triggers

Whereas social evaluation triggers are about how others perceive you, personal identity triggers are about how you perceive yourself. You recognize these threats as challenges to your competence, autonomy, purpose, or values. They call into question who you believe you are and what you stand for.

The following questions speak to your personal identity triggers. They can help you think through what triggers you when your sense of self feels attacked.

- How do you talk to yourself after failure?
- How do you react when not trusted to do your job?
- Do you find meaning in your daily life? What is it?
- What does it look like when someone disrespects your values?

On a scale of 1 (I'm nobody) to 5 (I'm awesome), how would you rate your sense of self?

On a scale of 1 (easygoing) to 5 (obsessive), how would you rate your need for control?

What do you notice about the difference between your answers to the previous two questions? What might this tell you about your personal identity triggers?

_____

_____

_____

_____

_____

_____

Your loss triggers

If social evaluation is about your perception of the other person and personal identity is about your self-perception, the loss trigger is about the relationship itself. You fear losing that connection. Loss triggers also occur when you fear losing a job or a status.

- What are you most afraid of losing? Your mind may initially think of *people* you're afraid to lose. That's normal and understandable, but not for this exercise. Instead, think of factors that give your own life meaning and purpose. For example:
    - Fear of losing an opportunity to advance in your field
    - Fear of losing progress or momentum toward a life goal
    - Fear of losing your current creature comforts to a new life change
    - _____
    - _____
    - _____
    - _____
    - _____

THE APPLICATION

- Rank the top five things you're most afraid of losing.

    1. _____
    2. _____
    3. _____
    4. _____
    5. _____

- When you feel the threat of loss, how do you react?

    - Overexplaining
    - Silence or hesitancy to speak
    - Withdrawal or avoidance
    - Other: _____

On a scale of 1 (little) to 5 (greatly), how much do you fear change?

1   2   3   4   5

On a scale of 1 (low) to 5 (high), how would you rate your fear of abandonment?

1   2   3   4   5

What do you notice about the difference between your answers to the previous two questions? What might this tell you about your loss triggers?

_____

_____

_____

_____

Understanding your unique triggers reveals where you can be proactive.

Now rank your triggers from 1 (top) to 3 (lowest).

    ___ Social evaluation

    ___ Personal identity

    ___ Loss

How does your top trigger most often reveal itself? (Remember: this is simply an exercise to spur thought!)

_____

_____

_____

What will you commit to do in your next conversation to decrease the severity of your response to that trigger?

_____

_____

_____

THE APPLICATION

Here's the cool part. When you better understand your triggers, you'll start to better identify what *triggers others*. You'll know that these aren't behaviors to get offended over but rather information to gather. Then you can leverage that information to bring cooling—even healing—to the conversation. You'll begin to hear someone's raised voice not as an attack but as a plea to remove the threat.

If you want to put out their fire, find their trigger.

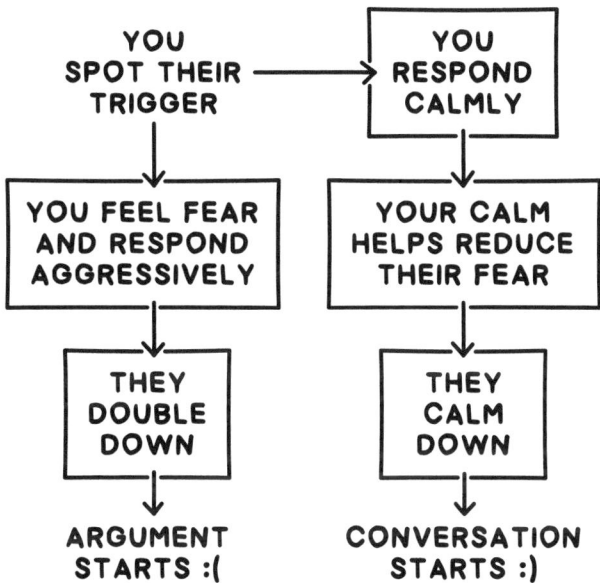

Putting It All Together

- Every argument has an ignition phase and a cooling phase.
- Your body automatically reacts during an argument.
- You have specific triggers that increase your reaction.

Knowing what you know now, what do you commit to do in your next argument? For instance:

The next time I feel my temperature rising in an argument, I will _____

_____.

The next time I experience another person's ignition phase, I will _____

_____.

The next time I see one of my triggers at work beneath the surface of an argument,

I will _____

_____.

What else would you add?

_____

_____

_____

When you take the time now to rationally think about how you'll approach your next argument, you'll be better prepared to control yourself no matter the circumstances.

Control the Moment

Chapter 5 in *The Next Conversation*

In the seconds before an argument begins, there's a brief moment when you can turn the tide in your favor.

No, this isn't about winning the argument. It's about steering the conversation. And if you're not careful, you'll miss your window.

Focusing on how you can beat the other person. Imagining the look on their face when you deliver your opening line or the perfect zinger. When you give in to these distractions, the conversation almost always sours. The end is nothing like you imagined. And neither person walks away feeling good.

But the outcome could be drastically different if, in that moment right before the argument, you make one choice: rather than looking to control the other person, you decide to control yourself.

To maintain control in an argument, remember these three mindsets:

1. Your first word is your breath.
2. Your first thought is a quick scan.
3. Your first conversation is a small talk.

This may seem like a lot to cram into just a few seconds before an argument ignites. But I promise you, with practice these steps will become second nature to you. And they will make a world of difference in your arguments and your relationships.

Your First Word Is Your Breath (*TNC*, pp. 95–103)

Whenever you're about to begin a sentence, let your *breath* be the first *word* you say. In other words, where your first word might be, put a breath in its place.

For example, your friend says, "I can't believe you'd vote for that person."

Your typical, immediate reply might be, "I can't believe you'd vote for *that* person." And just as quickly, an argument erupts (and no one changes anyone else's mind).

But when you choose to take a breath before replying, you'll often speak something truer, clearer, and less antagonistic. In the previous scenario, instead of sarcastically parroting what was said, let's say you take an intentional breath before speaking. This allows you to rethink your approach. Rather than going on offense, you choose to go on a fact-finding mission. In a measured tone, you ask, "Well, why can't you believe that?" Then a rational, considerate conversation can take place, even if it doesn't end in agreement.

Making your breath your first word is useful in all conversation, but it's especially powerful during conflict. Recall the earlier ignition and cooling phases. Incorporating purposeful breaths before you speak activates your cooling phase (and often theirs too) and brings rational thought into play. So while the other person may be starting from ignition temps, you're starting much cooler. Even if your temp rises, you won't boil over.

You're the objective referee to their angry head coach. You're the loving parent to their toddler tirade. You're the calm in the midst of their storm.

All because of a breath.

Do you believe that something as small and short as a breath can affect a conversation? Why or why not?

_____

_____

_____

On a scale of 1 (never) to 5 (always), how often do you take an intentional breath before a conversation?

1   2   3   4   5

Can you recall a time when intentional breathing helped you in an argument? If so, describe the moment. How did your breathing affect the outcome?

_____

_____

_____

How to take a conversational breath

Breathwork, breath control, controlled breathing, an intentional pause. To me, these all mean the same thing: purposefully using your breath to control the moment. I prefer to call it a conversational breath, because you can use it in the natural flow of your conversation. If this is new to you, you may feel awkward at first. But the more you use conversational breaths, the more natural it will seem. And you'll feel much more in control of yourself and of the conversation.

Here's how to take a conversational breath:

1. Breathe in slowly through your nose for two seconds.
2. At the top of the inhale, take another quick inhale through your nose for one second. The inhale count is now three.
3. Breathe out through your nose for six seconds, making your exhale about twice as long as your inhale.
4. Repeat the pattern at least twice, or as needed throughout the dialogue.

A conversational breath looks like this:

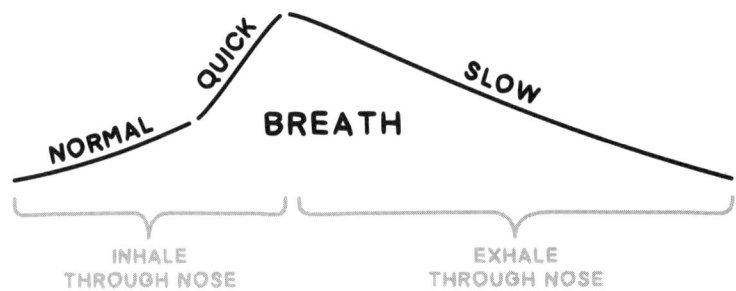

Now reread the previous steps and practice conversational breathing.

Try practicing it again but use a timer. Most people count too quickly. When you use a timer, you'll feel just how much of a difference nine seconds—the full length of a conversational breath—truly makes. Conversational breaths ensure that:

- Your breathing slows down. (Faster breathing is a signal of the ignition phase.)

- Your stress decreases. (Think about how you feel after a long sigh.)

- Your heart rate lessens. (Even if it slows just a little, you've told your body to relax.)

In other words, a conversational breath invites your cooling phase to the party before it's needed. And keep in mind, I'm not saying you need to take a full nine seconds before ever responding to someone. It's not a rigid rule. The more important point is that using the double inhale and exhale (for however long) activates your sense of calm and keeps your clarity.

Your First Thought Is a Quick Scan (*TNC*, pp. 103–110)

This second step works hand in hand with your conversational breath.

A quick scan is a mini-meditation to discover your body's stress points and your mind's anxieties. And it can make a world of difference in your response to others.

How to do a quick scan

While four steps are listed, with practice this will become a swift single step.

1. Begin your breath.
2. At the top of your inhalation, close your eyes briefly—like a long blink.
3. As you exhale, examine your body for hidden stress. Channel your exhalation into that part of your body and release its tension. Open your eyes.
4. Last, label your emotion in your mind. In one word, name what you're feeling.

A quick scan looks like this:

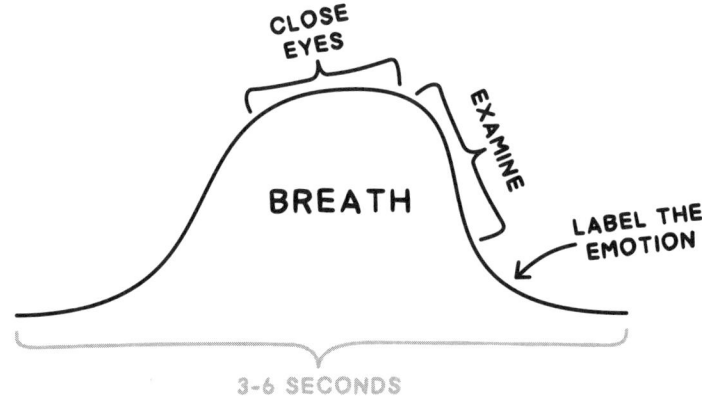

The first time you do a quick scan, you'll immediately feel its benefits: you de-stress, you gain control over your mind and body, and you become more self-aware of your reactions.

Practice a quick scan right now. Reread the previous steps. Take it slow.

Where did you find stress in your body? Label how each area feels on the illustration:

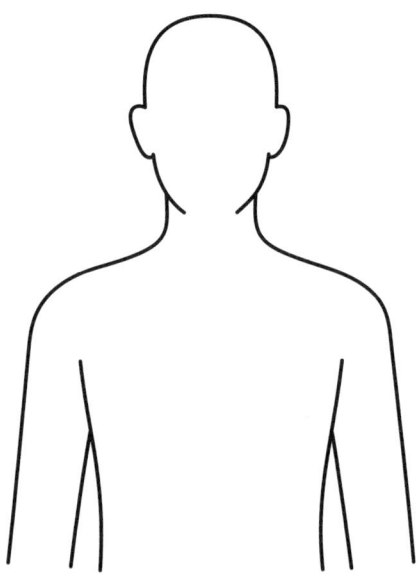

THE APPLICATION

Note: if you're in a relaxed state right now, consider doing this exercise as if you were in an argument.

When you labeled what you were feeling, what one word came to mind?

If you struggle to name your emotions, use weather terminology: *It's an overcast day. The clouds are dark. The sun is shining.* Once you've broadly described how you feel, try to pinpoint why you feel that way.

To translate your emotion into helpful words that let others know how you feel, begin your sentence with "I can tell . . ." For example, if you're angry, don't say, "I'm angry." Rather, say, "I can tell that I'm experiencing the feeling of anger." This gets the emotion out of your body and vulnerably lets the other person into your perspective without casting them as the bad guy.

When you follow your "I can tell" statement with what you need, you've made a strong case for yourself. Here are a few examples of emotions paired with "I can tell" statements. After reading the list, add your own emotion and statement to the end of the table.

Unhappy	"I can tell I'm not in the best mood. Can we please talk about this later?"
Threatened	"I can tell I'm feeling pressured right now. I need time to feel more secure."
Frustrated	"I can tell I'm getting frustrated. I need a time-out."
Anxious	"I can tell I'm not emotionally prepared for this conversation right now."

Unsettled	"I appreciate this conversation. I can tell there's more for me to process."
Overwhelmed	"I can tell I'm overwhelmed at the moment. Can we take this step-by-step?"
Confused	"I can tell I'm still confused about what you're saying. Could you say it to me differently?"
Nervous	"I can tell I'm a bit nervous about this decision. I need to go over the details again."
Sad	"I can tell I'm just feeling a little overcast. I need some time to myself right now."
Tired	"I can tell I'm not at my best right now. I need to revisit this after a break."

Done in tandem with your conversational breath, quick scans are the best way to grab hold of yourself, to discover what you're feeling, and to prepare yourself for the moment at hand.

Because when you claim it, you control it.

Your First Conversation Is a Small Talk (*TNC*, pp. 110–116)

You've controlled your internal reactions through a conversational breath. You've scanned your body to release your tension and name what you're feeling. Now you're going to find the courage to say exactly what you need to say through a small talk *with yourself.*

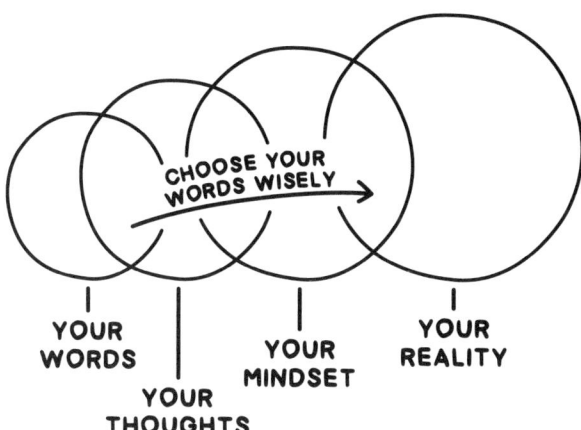

This final step in controlling the moment before an argument erupts requires just a second of your time. The more you practice it, the better and faster you'll get at it. Plus, we're going to build your small talk right now so you'll have it ready to go when you need it most.

A small talk is similar to a positive affirmation, but it's more concrete and tied to context. For example, affirmations like "I am loved" are great, but a small talk reminds you to do or be something.

- "Start with my breath."

- "Let the facts tell the truth."

- "Be true to your values."

Think of your small talk like receiving an encouraging text from a friend at the moment you need it, except the friend is you, reminding yourself of who you are and what you value.

To build a small talk, you need to know your goals and values. (See chapter two in *The Next Conversation*.)

Your goal for your next conversation should be reachable. Too often, we aim too high and feel disappointment when we miss the mark. Rather, an essential goal for every conversation should be to have something to learn, not something to prove.

From this foundation, you can add one more specific goal. The following questions can help you define that goal. Think about the next difficult conversation you may need to have with someone, then answer.

What's the one thing I need them to understand?

_____

What small step can I take to show them that I heard them?

_____

What assumptions am I making?

_____

_____

How can I show gratitude for this opportunity to talk?

_____

_____

Is there a part of this that I'm trying to win?

_____

_____

THE APPLICATION

Now that you know where you want the conversation to go, how do you get there?

Your conversational values are your compass. Let them guide your journey.

Rather than putting emphasis on the other person, your conversational values answer the question "How will I show up for myself?"

To discover your values, answer these questions:

- The last time I most felt like myself, my words and actions revealed the values of:

  _____

  _____

  _____

- When the conversation ends, who do I want to be seen as?

  _____

  _____

  _____

You may want to revisit what you learned from family and friends when you asked them about what you value (see p. 10 in this workbook). Just remember that you should tailor your general conversational values to the specific conversation you're about to have.

Reflect on what you've learned. In the space that follows, list the values you want to be known for—the legacy of character you want trailing in your wake.

These values can be a single word (*loyalty*) or a full sentence ("When it comes to relationships, I'm the person they can call at two a.m."). And you can have more than one.

_____

_____

_____

When you set your goals and values *before* your next conversation, you'll see your path and know your destination.

How to build your own small talk

Now let's use your goals and values to create your small talk.

Imagine you're about to have a difficult conversation with a close friend who seems to be pulling away from you.

What's your goal for the conversation? (Remember, this should be realistic and reachable, not improbable and unattainable.)

_____

_____

What value(s) will you bring to the conversation?

_____

_____

THE APPLICATION

To create your small talk:

- **Tie it to your goal.** Your small talks will always be different because they depend on the goal of the conversation. For example, if your goal is to be confident, your small talk might be "Voice it." If your goal is to refrain from igniting, your small talk might be "Seek to understand."

- **Start with a verb.** An active word leads to an active mindset. Instead of *being* something ("I am strong"), you're *doing* something ("Stand up"). Verbs prompt behavior. If you're going to control the moment, you need to *do* something about it.

- **Make it short and personal.** You're the only one hearing your small talk, and you need only to quickly remind yourself of your goal. When your small talk is deeply personal, like a memory, your body and mind will resonate with the feeling of that memory. Maybe it's something a grandparent said to you when you were a child. Maybe it's the encouragement you received from your boss last week. Use these phrases as anchors during self-doubt or hesitation.

For example, if your goal is confidence, your small talk could be "Keep your head up." For more inspiration, see pp. 115–116 in *The Next Conversation*.

So, your friend is pulling away from you.

You know you need to talk about it for the sake of the friendship.

What will you say to yourself in the moments before that conversation?

_____

_____

Putting It All Together

In the span of just a few seconds, these three strategies will help you control the moment that too many people let pass by.

- Your first word is your breath.
- Your first thought is a quick scan.
- Your first conversation is a small talk.

Which of these strategies might be the most difficult for you to consistently use? Why?

_____

_____

_____

What will you commit to do so that this process becomes second nature?

_____

_____

_____

Control the Pace

Chapter 6 in *The Next Conversation*

You can make all the preparations in the world and still find yourself struggling in the heat of a conversation.

You can control yourself long before an argument erupts. You can use a conversational breath, a quick scan, and a small talk in the seconds before you speak. But then, when the talk gets going, the wheels fall off. The other person makes a detour you didn't expect. They swerve or speed up. Then you lose your bearings or you lose your cool. You think, *Why did I ever listen to Jefferson?*

If you'll bear with me, there's one more step to saying it with control: managing the pace of a conversation. Even if you're soft-spoken, you can use the following steps to have a calm, deliberate presence in every conversation.

The Gift of a Pause (*TNC*, pp. 121–127)

Our tendency as humans is to talk faster when we're anxious, scared, or upset. Like fire seeking oxygen, it's your ignition phase finding its escape through your mouth. Physically speaking, you can't help yourself—unless you choose to become consciously aware of what your body is doing. After all, when you speak quickly, you're often not speaking rationally. You're reacting in the moment instead of using the moment to steer the conversation.

Think about the way your conversations typically go. This includes average conversations and the ones that get heated. On a scale of 1 (rarely) to 5 (most of the time), grade yourself on the following statements:

___ I think about my response while the other person is still talking.

___ I cut people off in conversation.

___ I stumble over my words.

___ I put my foot in my mouth.

___ I run out of breath during heated conversations.

___ I can't control the direction of a conversation.

Add up your numbers. If your total is above 20, you might be someone who tends to overexplain or feels the need to add a lot of context. People who are neurodivergent or have conditions like ADHD tend to have high scores. If your total is below 15, you may be someone who has a difficult time speaking up for themselves or whose default is to people please.

When you feel yourself speeding up, do you believe you have any control over the conversation? Why or why not?

_____

_____

The truth is that you're *not* just along for the ride. Your foot's been hovering above your brake the entire time. You just need to push it.

A well-timed pause in conversation is your most effective tool to fix your communication problems.

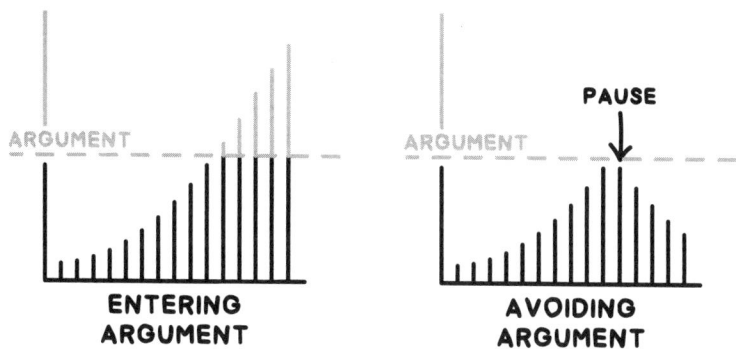

Does that make you worry? In the following list, check all of your fears when it comes to using more pauses in your conversation.

"If I slow my talking and/or use more pauses, I'll feel . . .":

☐ Weird

☐ Incompetent

☐ Unprepared

☐ Uncaring

☐ Uncertain

☐ Impatient

☐ Weak

☐ Other: _____

When you leverage the power of the pause, others will notice. The gift of the pause is the ability to control time.

What benefits could you enjoy by choosing a deliberate pace and more pauses in your conversations? (For my answers, see pp. 124–127 in *The Next Conversation*.)

Slowness isn't softness. Silence isn't weakness. Used purposefully, they are powerful tools of confidence and self-control.

How and When to Use Pauses (*TNC*, pp. 127–133)

The length of a pause determines its meaning. Just think of the difference between your friend's responding to your text in five minutes versus five days. Their text may use the same words, but the response time communicates a different message (whether intended or not).

So, when choosing to use more pauses in your conversation, think about which type of pause the situation calls for.

- **Short pauses are reading glasses.** Lasting one to four seconds, a short pause brings emphasis and focus—like putting on glasses to read the fine print.

- **Long pauses are mirrors.** Lasting five to ten seconds, a long pause provides time for reflection *for both parties*—like looking into a mirror.

Think about the last time a friend, spouse, or coworker asked you a question and you immediately snapped back. What did they ask? And what was your response? What adjectives would you use to describe your response?

_____

_____

_____

_____

THE APPLICATION

Replay that moment in your mind and insert a four-second pause between their question and your answer. What adjectives describe your response after a short pause?

_____

_____

_____

_____

Hopefully, you can see the difference between a terse reply and a reasoned response—even if you use the same words. When you place a pause between any words that threaten your ignition phase and your response, you take the heat out of the room. You de-risk the conversation before it's even begun.

Short pauses are just as useful in casual conversation. Take the typical greeting "How are you?" Most of us will immediately reply, "I'm good," or "Doing great!" or "Too blessed to be stressed." But when you place a short pause before your answer, the same words can convey that you've considered your answer. The pause also shows that you're respecting the other person's interest in you. And it seeks connection over transaction.

Short pauses also add emphasis on just the right . . . word. If you really need to stress a phrase or word, let a pregnant pause of a second or two hang in the air right before you say what they need to hear.

Remember too: a short pause is a perfect time for your first word to be your breath.

In your next conversation, use a purposeful pause. Maybe even count off a second or two in your head as you're doing it. Then try a pause that's three or four seconds long.

My hope is that you begin to feel the actual length of a short pause. Even short pauses can feel like they take forever, especially in heated conversations, but that's when you need them most. By practicing pausing right now, you're preparing yourself for that day.

If you really want to experience the power of a pause, listen to a talented orator like Martin Luther King Jr. to see how he pauses for effect.

There's power . . . in the pause. Use it.

Putting It All Together

When you become comfortable with "awkward" pauses, you will be amazed at the breakthroughs that happen in your conversations and relationships.

When you give a conversation room to breathe, you provide space for the other person to hear their words echo back to them. If they're bullying or joking, your pause deflates their words. If they're accusing or judging, your pause lets them assess their words. If they're arguing or igniting, your pause allows cooler air to descend.

I promise you: there's power in the pause.

In chapter eight of *The Next Conversation*, I offer more specific pause techniques when speaking with someone who seeks to hurt you verbally. For now, here's what I encourage you to do.

- **Start using short pauses today.** You don't have to start big. Begin with short pauses, the conversational reading glasses that emphasize what you want to say and how you want to say it.

- **Then add long pauses.** You could even consider counting in your head—one, two, three, four—so that you're giving your conversation the space it needs.

Practice both kinds of pauses enough times so that you begin to see what a difference they make.

Rule 1 Review

Fill in the following blanks. On your first pass, try to fill in what you remember. On your second pass, go back through the sections and fill in any words you may have missed. Circle any of the steps that you want to start using today in your life and conversations.

Rule 1: Say it with _____.

- Control _____.

    – The two phases of every argument are _____ and _____.

    – Psychological triggers arrive in three ways:

        * _____ triggers

        * _____ triggers

        * _____ triggers

- Control _____.

    – Your first _____ is your _____.

    – Your first _____ is a _____.

    – Your first _____ is a _____.

THE APPLICATION

- Control _____.

  - _____ pauses are _____.

  - _____ pauses are _____.

  - There's _____ in the pause.

Extra note space:

THE APPLICATION

RULE 2

Say It with Confidence

Um, uh, I'd just like to . . .
   Well, I mean, you know . . .
   Basically, what I'm trying to say is . . .
Know what I mean?

Imagine reading a book like that. You'd set it down just as soon as you'd picked it up. You can tell that the author lacks confidence. And if they don't believe in their words, why should you?

Yet this is how many of us speak. We think we're being humble or kind or deferential, but the truth is that we're not standing up for ourselves. And we're decreasing our believability.

If you don't believe in your words, why should anyone else?

To change your life for the better, let's discover your confidence. The only way to feel more confident is to live it out more fully. It's an active process that you build and accumulate by engaging in specific behaviors.

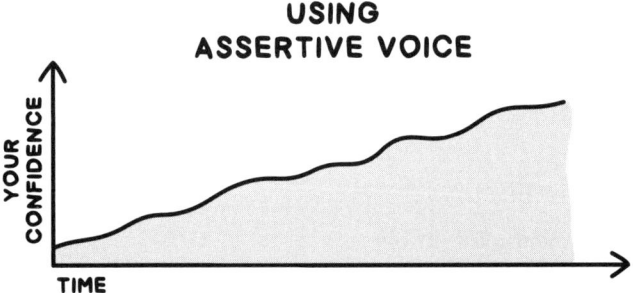

This section covers the confidence-building behaviors that anyone can learn and adopt.

- Find your assertive voice.
- Stand your ground with difficult people.
- Establish your boundaries.

When you make these behaviors a consistent part of your conversations, you're building the muscles that your confidence needs so your inner strength is always ready for action.

On a scale of 1 (meek) to 5 (confident), rate your average confidence level in conversations.

Whom in your life do you admire for their confidence? How does their confidence reveal itself?

_____

_____

In what areas of your life do you wish you had more confidence?

_____

_____

How would having more confidence change your life or relationships? Be specific.

_____

_____

Assertive Voice

Chapter 7 in *The Next Conversation*

You can't just feel confident at will. You have to experience moments when you can exercise your confidence. That exercising—the doing of confidence—is called assertiveness. If confidence is the feeling, assertiveness is the action. To assert yourself is confidence in motion.

When you assert yourself, you feel more confident. When you feel more confident, you assert yourself more. The pair forms a positive feedback loop, a flywheel set in perpetual motion.

In the following pages, we'll discuss ten ways to practice assertiveness—plus a subtle bonus strategy that could make all the difference. Because there are so many strategies here, this is the longest section of the workbook. Don't try the strategies all at once. Focus on one tactic you can apply to your next conversation. As you become comfortable with that step, then add another.

The goal isn't to check off a to-do list of assertiveness. The goal is to launch your flywheel.

Every Word Matters (*TNC*, pp. 141–142)

Assertiveness has its own language, both in what to say and what not to say. Of all the assertive strategies I share, nothing matters more than word choice. This is true for conversations with a friend or emails with your boss. What you say or type—every word of it—matters.

If all another person knew about you was based on your words, how would they describe you?

_____

_____

_____

_____

_____

Let's consider how a few simple edits transform hesitancy into assertiveness. In the examples that follow, strike out the words that show a lack of confidence.

- "To be honest, I think my skills will be an asset to your company."
- "I actually think that you probably shouldn't."
- "I just want to touch base a bit."

Here's what I would remove. Read these out loud to hear the difference even these small changes make.

- "~~To be honest, I think~~ my skills will be an asset to your company."

- "~~I actually think that~~ you probably shouldn't."

- "I ~~just~~ want to touch base ~~a bit~~."

In the following columns, check every word or phrase you commonly use that undercuts your assertiveness.

☐	Just	☐	Does that make sense?
☐	I think	☐	I hate to bother you, but . . .
☐	I guess	☐	Sorry
☐	I feel	☐	Sort of
☐	I might	☐	Kind of
☐	Know what I mean?		

The next time you want to speak one of these words, replace it with a breath.

Prove It to Yourself (*TNC*, pp. 142–145)

Claim your words, then fulfill your words. By this I mean state your intent and stay true to the promise you've made to yourself.

This statement always begins with *I* and a present-tense verb. For example, "I'm moving forward from this conversation."

Say it out loud, then follow through. If you don't actually "move forward from this conversation," you've hollowed out your own words. You've minimized your voice.

While the other person needs to hear your intent, hearing yourself offers the better benefit. You're proving to yourself that you're a person of your word.

When did you last say a word of intention but didn't follow through? What caused you not to act on your intention?

_____

_____

_____

How do you think the other person viewed you as a result?

_____

_____

_____

How did you view yourself in that moment? What do you wish you would have done differently?

_____

_____

_____

What was the dynamic with that person the next time you spoke with them?

_____

_____

In which areas of your life, or with which people, do you need to be more intentional in confidently stating your next step and then taking it?

_____

_____

_____

These small, assertive actions will build your confidence. And they are all the more important for establishing a strong foundation when it comes to enforcing your boundaries, the focus of chapter nine in *The Next Conversation*.

Express Your Needs Unapologetically (*TNC*, pp. 145–148)

Advocating for yourself means being your own lawyer. You speak confident truth on your client's behalf, knowing that no one else is going to plead their case. Because you know what they need, your words are strong, deliberate, and clear. When the other side makes their demands, you reply, "My client won't accept that."

To express your needs unapologetically, replace *my client* with *I*: "I won't accept that."

In the same vein, make "I need . . ." an essential phrase in your vocabulary. Set your default to stating your needs. For example, "I need you to hear me." This simple shift empowers you to own your wants and communicate them clearly. You're choosing to stand up for your client-self.

Bring to mind your last conversation when you didn't feel heard or understood. If you were playing lawyer for yourself—an outside observer who just wants to help that person stand up for themselves—what would you say on your behalf? (Begin your defense with "My client . . .")

"My client _____."

Now edit your statement so that it's in the first person.

_____

Now speak it out loud. How does it make you feel to make it personal? To say it?

_____

One more tip: do all of this *unapologetically*. That means ridding yourself of another crutch phrase you think is kindness or, at worst, harmless. But it's harming you more than you know.

The phrase is *I'm sorry*.

Look at it this way. Would an attorney pleading their client's case ever begin their argument with "I'm sorry, judge, but . . ."?

Save "I'm sorry" for when it matters. Instead of over-apologizing, use words of gratitude. For example, turn "Sorry I'm late" into "Thank you for your patience."

Practice this transformation by completing these before-and-after examples:

Before: "Sorry to bother you."

After: _____

Before: "Sorry for all the questions."

After: _____

Before: "I'm sorry, can you repeat that?"

After: _____

Silence is a better response than over-apologizing.

Saying that you're sorry too often reveals a lack of self-esteem. Your self-worth isn't tied to how little an inconvenience you can be. Never be sorry that you're a human who also has needs and wants.

Speak When It Matters
(*TNC*, pp. 148–150)

Why is it that the person who has the least to contribute often has the most to say? Or that the person with the most to offer says the least?

Because insecure people feel pressured to prove themselves through their many words. It's all smoke and mirrors, no substance.

But confident people have nothing to prove. They trust themselves without regard to external validation. They listen. They wait to speak. And they say only what they need to say.

For the most confident person you know, does their character fit the stereotype of knowing the most but saying the least? How do they present themselves in words and actions?

_____

_____

What would need to change in your conversations to talk less but say more?

_____

_____

Is that a change you're willing to make? If so, how will you make that change tomorrow?

_____

_____

Say Less (*TNC*, pp. 150–151)

If you're going to speak only when it matters, you'll naturally say less. But there's another lesson here: the fewer the words, the clearer the point.

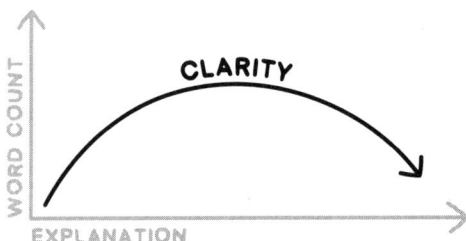

When you flood the market of conversation with excessive words, you create a deficit of attention. As your word count goes up, your listener's interest goes down. Plus, overexplaining shows a lack of confidence. The longer you speak, the less believable you sound.

Rather, with fewer words, each word increases in value. The other person will pay more attention. And your efficiency of language will reveal a quiet confidence.

On a scale of 1 (never) to 5 (always), how often do you feel the need to fill silence?

If you're at 3 or above, why does silence bother you? Be specific.

_____

_____

If you're at 2 or under, why do you allow silence? Be specific.

_____

_____

Remove Filler Words (*TNC*, pp. 151–152)

We subconsciously use filler words to fill the gaps of conversation. In casual conversation they're harmless. But in professional settings they can be confidence killers. These words and phrases are close cousins to the confidence-eroding words we've already covered, but they are much subtler.

In the list that follows, check your most-used filler words. If you're unsure, ask a close friend. (You may not even be aware of how often you use these words.)

- ☐ Um
- ☐ Uh
- ☐ Like
- ☐ You know
- ☐ Okay

- ☐ Right
- ☐ Yeah
- ☐ Hmm
- ☐ Other: _____

Note: *and*, *but*, and *so* are necessary conjunctions, but if they're used too often, they can also be filler words.

For a real challenge, record a ten-minute casual conversation between you and your friend (with their consent, of course). Talk about whatever you'd like. A week later, listen to the recording and track how often you say any filler words.

By now you should know the solution to filler words: replace them with silence. When you first begin this practice, try saying the filler word in your mind but let it come out of your mouth as a breath.

If you want to sound assertive, serve your words neat.

Never Undersell (*TNC*, pp. 152–155)

The only person who sets your value is you. So don't begin your conversations by undercutting your worth at the very start. Phrases that undersell your value (and slowly eat away at your confidence) include "I hate to bother you," "Forgive me for the dumb question," and "Does that make sense?"

This is self-doubt masquerading as humility or kindness. Of course be kind to others and humble when it's called for—but not at the expense of your intrinsic value to a relationship or conversation. Don't start conversations by digging a hole beneath your feet.

What words or phrases have you caught yourself using that undersell your value?

_____

_____

_____

_____

_____

The next time you're about to downplay your presence, pause and consider one of two options:

1. Replace it with silence; or
2. Rephrase your thought assertively.

For example, "Does that make sense?" could become "What are your thoughts?" The goal is to build upon or break down the issue at hand.

Transform your underselling phrases from the previous question by removing the self-doubt and using assertive words. (Remember: whenever you're at a loss, start with *I* plus a present-tense verb.)

Cut the Excess (*TNC*, pp. 155–156)

Let's briefly return to elementary English class. Adverbs describe verbs and most often end in *-ly*, as in "She communicated *confidently*." They're *perfectly* fine in casual conversation. But when you want to sound strong, the first budget cut in your economy of words should be your adverbs.

In the list that follows, check the adverbs you often use.

- ☐ Just
- ☐ So
- ☐ Very
- ☐ Only
- ☐ Too
- ☐ Like
- ☐ Actually
- ☐ Basically

- ☐ Essentially
- ☐ Literally
- ☐ Definitely
- ☐ Extremely
- ☐ Truly
- ☐ Really
- ☐ Most
- ☐ Other: _____

You know the drill by now. To make an impact, drop your adverbs. In the following example, cross out every adverb:

Hey, so I essentially just like really wanted to say how truly grateful I am for quite literally everything you've done for me lately.

Now write the previous sentence without the adverbs:

___

When in Doubt, Fall Back on Experience
(*TNC*, pp. 156–157)

When you're asked a question that you don't have an answer to, rely on your experiences. Use phrases like "I haven't come across this before" or "In the past, I've . . ." As you remember, you may discover the answer you need. Even if a firm answer doesn't come to mind, you've at least given the other person more than a shrug of your shoulders.

There's also no harm in admitting "I don't know." Such an answer shows honesty and humility that can build trust. You can also say, "I don't know, but I'll find out." But make sure that your intent matches your result. When you find out, get back to that person.

The goal isn't to just have something to say in reply. The goal is to provide value to the conversation and relationship. You're not just casually dismissing the other person. Rather, you're giving a reasoned response—even if you don't have an immediate answer.

Recall a time when you had to fall back on your experiences in a conversation. What did the other person ask? What did you share?

___

_____

_____

Did your answer provide value? (Remember: value isn't limited to answering their direct question.)

_____

_____

_____

Say "I'm Confident" (*TNC*, pp. 157–158)

This gets right to the point, both for you and the other person. Before giving an answer, preface it with "I'm confident." By just speaking the words, you'll feel more confident. And in hearing the words, the other person will associate confidence with you.

For example, *"I believe I can help"* puts on serious muscle when it becomes *"I'm confident I can help."*

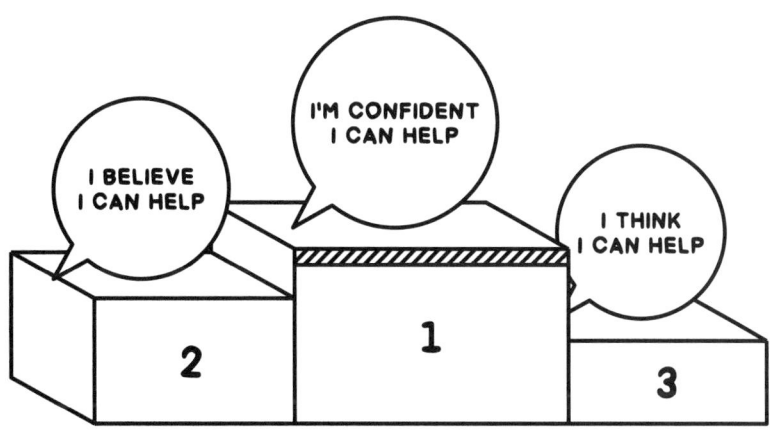

When someone else says, "I think . . ." or "I believe . . ." or "I guess . . . ," how do you typically view them? Check all the words you associate with that kind of speaking.

- ☐ Wishy-washy
- ☐ Unsure
- ☐ Ignorant
- ☐ Unconfident
- ☐ Doubtful
- ☐ Shy
- ☐ Anxious
- ☐ Nervous
- ☐ Apprehensive
- ☐ Insecure
- ☐ Scared
- ☐ Self-conscious
- ☐ Other: _____

From 1 (least) to 5 (most), rank how often you use these top confidence-killing phrases.

___ I think

___ I believe

___ I guess

___ I suppose

___ I might

In addition to bluntly saying "I'm confident," the following assertive phrases will also strengthen your belief in yourself and in your words.

- Here's what I know.
- Let's move forward.

- That's not an option.
- In my experience, I . . .
- I trust that we will find what's right.
- I stand by that.
- I'd like to change direction.
- I've considered it.
- I'm comfortable with / I'm not comfortable with . . .
- I've decided to . . .

Mind Your Tone (*TNC*, pp. 158–161)

The *sound* of confidence is essential. You may have removed every unnecessary word from your speech, but if you say the important words in the wrong tone, what was the point?

Here's the bonus strategy: to be assertive, seek a balanced tone.

It's like wearing headphones where the volume is just right in each ear.

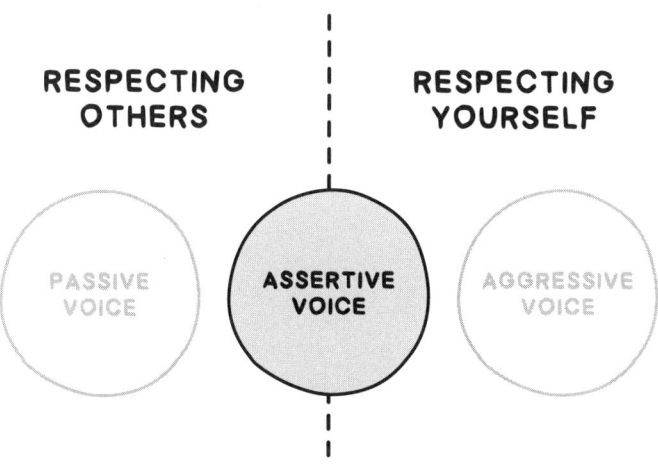

You can also think of it on a spectrum:

On that spectrum, where does your conversational tone most often hang out? Mark it with an X.

To achieve more balance, avoid uptalk—the tendency to end your words or sentences with an upward inflection. Ending on a vocal upswing signals uncertainty or approval seeking. Both undermine your assertiveness.

So when you're inclined to go high, choose to go low or stay neutral. Choose a balanced conversational tone. The difference is minimal but immense.

If this is a persistent issue for you, practice it at home alone. I'm not saying you should sound robotic, but you may want to take lessons from your digital personal assistant. Don't they always sound confident (even when they're wrong)?

To increase your assertiveness, mind your cadence as well as your tone. Speaking too fast signals nervousness. Too slow shows uncertainty. But a measured, controlled pace plus a balanced tone proves that you know what you're about.

One last tip: make eye contact. It shows engagement, sincerity, confidence, and respect. Don't stare, but don't avoid looking the other person in the eye altogether either. Balance is the key. If this is an issue for you, wait to make eye contact until the last few words of your sentence. End with the eyes.

When it comes to tone, pace, or eye contact, which do you need to focus on most?

___

How will you put intention in your tone, pace, or eye contact in your next conversation? Be specific.

_____

_____

_____

_____

Putting It All Together

Consider this section like spaghetti. I threw a lot at you. Stick with what sticks.

If you've read this far and you're still struggling to identify where your words are getting in the way of your wants and needs, print out your last several emails or text messages. Then strike out all the words or phrases (*just*, *like*, *guess*, etc.) that are subtly making you "less than" in the eyes of others.

Now you're ready for this self-assessment. In the following list, sequentially rank the areas you should focus on from 1 ("I need help") to 11 ("I've got this").

____ Stop using words that undercut my assertiveness.

____ State my intentions and stay true to my promises.

____ Express my needs unapologetically.

____ Speak when it matters.

____ Say less.

____ Remove filler words.

___ Stop underselling myself.

___ Cut the adverbs.

___ Fall back on my experiences.

___ Say "I'm confident."

___ Mind my tone, pace, and eye contact.

Now, for your top-ranked issue, how will you commit to focusing on that in your next conversation? Be specific.

_____

_____

_____

_____

What do you fear will happen when you start using these strategies?

_____

_____

_____

THE APPLICATION

After a week or two of using your newfound assertive voice, answer these questions:

How did you feel when you asserted yourself?

_____

_____

_____

How did the other person react?

_____

_____

_____

Once you feel confident in one strategy, add another. (You now have a handy list to help.) Keep building your assertiveness vocabulary so that you'll never struggle to find the right words—the clear, strong, and confident words—exactly when you need them.

Difficult People

Chapter 8 in *The Next Conversation*

Your family, friends, and coworkers—the people you're close to and who know you the best—can often inflict the most damage. They know your weak points. Like a bully in a schoolyard, they attack with precision. They're called *cutting remarks* for a reason.

In the moment after the attack, your fight-or-flight response comes to your defense. You think you have two choices: retreat or push back harder. But there's a better option in the heat of the moment: using your new assertive voice to create responses that leave no room for misinterpretation, responses that have all the boldness of aggression with none of the disrespect.

Similar to the previous section, there's a lot to learn here. Don't try to retain it all at once. Focus on the areas you may need to work on most. When you feel confident and capable in that area, choose a new one. Little by little, you'll begin to hear the words you've always wanted to say coming out of your mouth—showing greater respect for yourself and without disrespecting the other person.

Let's dig into what to say when someone insults you, apologizes poorly, or interrupts you.

When They Insult or Offend You (*TNC*, pp. 167–169)

Think about the last time someone insulted you or offended you in person. What did they say or do?

_____

_____

_____

How did you respond? Write down what you said, your body language, and how you felt.

_____

_____

_____

What do you wish you would have done differently?

_____

_____

_____

When another person is insulting or offensive, they say they're "just trying to get a rise" out of us. The truth is that they're trying to get a rise within themselves: a kick of dopamine. Once they get their hit—especially if you react the way they hope—they need to keep getting their fix. So the cycle continues until you choose to stand up for yourself and stop giving them what they're seeking.

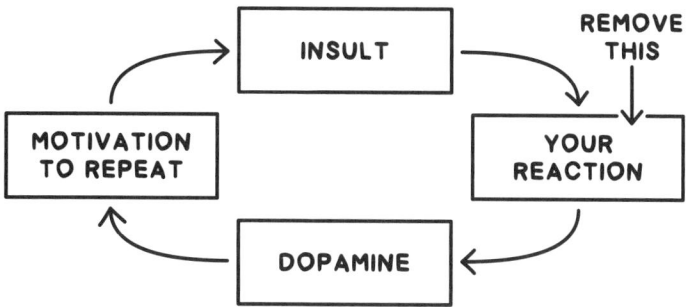

When someone insults or offends you, here's how to remove what they want.

1. **Give it a long pause.** This pause is more for their benefit than for yours. When someone says, "You don't know anything," and you pause, their words echo back to them and you remove their instant dopamine reward.

2. **Slowly repeat what they said.** If silence doesn't work, slowly say, "I don't know anything?" Use a calm, measured tone. This could feel even more awkward than the silence, but it's powerful evidence against the other person of how ridiculous they're sounding. In this step, you're literally their echo.

3. **Keep breathing out.** At this point, their ignition phase may go nuclear or their cooling phase may start. Either way, *breathe*. Relax. You've resisted giving them their fix so far, so don't give in now. Depending on their response, you may also need to assert a boundary (the subject of the next section).

What do you fear will happen when you use these steps the next time someone insults you?

When They Belittle, Patronize, or Condescend to You
(*TNC*, pp. 169–171)

How have you experienced belittling, patronizing, or condescending behavior in the past? Write down the words and actions that come to mind.

How did you typically respond?

THE APPLICATION

Why did you respond that way?

_____

_____

_____

At least insults are direct. Belittling, patronizing, or condescending remarks often come cloaked in friendliness. They may be said jokingly, but you and the other person know what was intended. They want to "put you in your place" and make you feel insecure—all with a smile on their face. These steps can help them see that it's no laughing matter.

1. **Make them say it again.** If they say "Great job" in that sarcastic way you've heard a hundred times before, reply with, "I need you to repeat that." This way you're throwing the spotlight back on them. If they want to be center stage, let them shine.

2. **Ask a question of outcome.** If a reply or an apology doesn't arrive, ask a question that highlights what they were hoping to achieve, e.g., "Did that feel good to say out loud?" Be the echo that they're too high and mighty to hear.

3. **Reply with silence.** (Notice a trend?) Regardless of how they answer your question, say nothing in return. In most cases, they'll make an excuse for their behavior ("I was just joking") or take further offense ("Really? You're giving me grief for that?"). When you say nothing, you let their poor behavior be the reply they need. And they won't soon forget that the next time they want to sarcastically tell you "Great job."

What do you fear will happen when you use these steps the next time someone belittles, patronizes, or condescends to you?

_____

When They're Rude or Dismissive (*TNC*, pp. 171–172)

When were you last shocked by someone's rudeness? This can be an experience of your own or one you witnessed. Describe what happened and what was said.

_____

Why was the experience shocking?

_____

When someone is rude to you or dismisses your perspective, how do you respond?

___

___

___

For me, rude and dismissive remarks sit in the middle of the spectrum of disrespectful comments. They're not as subtle as belittling or as overt as insults. Consequently, we tend to dismiss dismissive remarks. But just as every word matters in what you say, every disrespectful word you allow from another person matters, both to your own strong sense of self and in how the other person perceives you. So the next time someone is rude to you, choose to respond like this:

1. **Give it a short pause.** While this is still effective for the other person to hear what they've just said, this pause is more for your sake. In this moment, you get to decide whether what they've said is worth your time and effort. Sometimes the best reply to a dismissive remark is no reply at all.

2. **Ask a question of intent.** This question isn't about outcome but rather input, e.g., "Was that meant to be helpful or hurtful?" Remember: throw the spotlight back at them.

3. **Wait.** In the awkward, fidgety silence, the other person may apologize, clarify, or dig in. If they reply well, you've shown that you're not afraid to stand up for yourself, even in the "little" things. If they dig in, you move on. You have better things to do with your time.

What do you fear will happen when you use these steps the next time someone is rude or dismissive toward you?

_____

_____

_____

Here's a cheat sheet for how to respond to insults, belittling, and rudeness. Maybe someone in your life always says something to you that you know you should respond to differently. Take time now to consider how you might respond to them the next time they make *that* remark. The three blank lines at the end are for you to fill in your own answers.

When they say:	Their goal is:	Respond with:
"You're an idiot."	to insult you	"I'm an idiot?"
"I knew you wouldn't get it right."	to belittle you	"Did that feel good to say out loud?"
"No, you're wrong."	to dismiss you	"Did you mean for that to come across as dismissive?"

THE APPLICATION

Pushing Back Against Bad Apologies (*TNC*, pp. 172–177)

How often do you receive an excuse disguised as an apology?

You know the kind. Without question, the other person has hurt you in some way. They know it too; otherwise, they wouldn't be trying to backtrack with a bad apology. So they say something—"I'm sorry, I'm just stressed"—that they hope takes the blame off their shoulders.

But it's not a real apology. There's no specificity. There's no promise to change. There's no reconciliation. It's just words to make them feel better about having made you feel worse. The more you accept bad apologies, the more of them you'll receive. While there's nothing you can do to force someone to apologize, you can stand up for yourself and let it be known that you will no longer be accepting bad, useless apologies. Here's how:

The following table shows these common "apologies," what the other person says, and how you can respond. Note how in each example you're turning the spotlight back on them and you're keying in on the words they're using.

Type	They say:	You reply:
No-empathy apology	"I'm sorry you feel that way."	"Don't apologize for my feelings; apologize for what you did."
No-apology apology	"I'm sorry if I did something wrong." "I'm sorry if I upset you."	"I need you to change the *if* to *that*."
Excuse apology	"I'm sorry. I've just been so stressed."	"You don't need to apologize for your stress. I need you to apologize for your words."

Type	They say:	You reply:
Toxic apology	"I'm sorry that I'm so horrible." "I'm sorry that you're perfect."	"I'm willing to accept an apology."
Justification apology	"I was just kidding."	"Then be funnier." "I wasn't."

Which type of "apology" have you heard lately? (You may have even been the one to give it. We're all guilty of using these at some point.)

_____

_____

Which "apology" really gets under your skin? Why?

_____

_____

What do you fear will happen when you use one of these replies? If it helps, imagine a scenario with your best friend giving you one of these types of "apologies." You respond with one of the listed replies. What happens next?

_____

_____

THE APPLICATION

_____

_____

_____

The End of Interruptions (*TNC*, pp. 177–181)

Interruptions in casual conversation are to be expected. But what about those moments when you're trying to make an impact? Maybe it's a business meeting or a heart-to-heart. Maybe you just need the other person to hear you for once. In those moments, you need to know how to handle interruptions so that you maintain the high ground.

1. **Let the other person interrupt you.** Only do this once. When they've finished their thought, resume from where you left off. Don't address their comment.

2. **Use their name.** If they interrupt again, say their name out loud at a normal level. If they don't stop, repeat it while increasing your volume. Stay calm.

3. **Correct the behavior.** Assert yourself with *I*-driven statements:
   - "I cannot hear you when you interrupt me."
   - "I'll listen to you when I'm finished."
   - "I want to listen to you. I need to finish my thought before I do."

By using these steps, you've remained rational, calm, and in control—both of yourself and of the situation. You've asserted your right to be heard and respected.

And the people in the room won't soon forget that.

The way someone handles interruptions often reveals what they think of themselves. Whether out of kindness or meekness, some will allow others to trample their words. Whether out of insecurity or aggression, others will engage in a shouting match. When you choose this third way, where you stand up for yourself without disrespecting others, you prove to yourself that you're a confident person who deserves to be heard.

How do you typically handle interruptions?

_____

_____

How was this modeled for you? (E.g., do you handle interruptions the same way your parents did?)

_____

_____

_____

Does the way you handle interruptions align with your conversational goals and values?

_____

_____

_____

What do you fear will happen when you choose to handle your next interruption this way?

___

___

___

___

A Better Way to Disagree (*TNC*, pp. 181–187)

Winning an argument is like winning a board game. You get a quick hit of dopamine but then what? Nothing really changes. In fact, winning an argument often loses you more.

But disagreements happen. Arguments erupt. So how can you learn to disagree effectively? To speak your mind without losing your relationships? Try these strategies.

Apply the *Is it worth it?* filter

This is straightforward. As soon as you understand the issue at hand, ask yourself, "Is this argument worth my time, energy, or focus?"

Out loud, you can say, "Is this something we have to agree on?" The issue may be important to the other person, but asking about agreement forces the other person to evaluate the priority of the conversation.

Let's make this practical. In the following list of issues to argue about, rank them from 1 (not worth it) to 10 (worth it). Of course, these issues are context dependent, but rank them according to your current state of mind.

___ How to load the dishwasher

___ Who to vote for

___ Where to eat dinner

___ What kind of school to send the kids to

___ What kind of job to have

___ Whether to be on social media

___ How often to visit relatives

___ What the household budget should be

___ What movie to watch

___ How your friend or significant other dresses

Now, what if the other person says, "Yes, we need to agree on this"?

Reply with, "Is this something we have to agree on *now*?" This forces the other person to evaluate the timing of the conversation. (Have you ever been almost entirely asleep in bed and then your spouse says something like, "What do you think about sending the kids to private school?")

By adding *now*, you're helping the other person assess whether this moment is the best moment to discuss what's important to them. Maybe you need more information. Maybe you need more *sleep*. Either way, you're still respecting them by showing that you want to discuss the issue—just not right now.

Think about the people you're closest to. Name three of them, then briefly describe a disagreement you recently had with them. It can be mundane or consequential.

THE APPLICATION

_____

_____

Were most of your disagreements over the small things or the large things? Why do you think that was the case?

_____

_____

_____

Choose one of those disagreements and retroactively apply the *Is it worth it?* filter. Was the argument worth your time, energy, or focus? Was it worth it at that exact moment?

_____

_____

_____

What do you fear may happen to your arguments when you use the *Is it worth it?* filter—especially when the argument is with a close loved one?

_____

_____

_____

_____

_____

Use your vantage point

Opt for phrases that signal viewpoints, not verdicts. For example, when you say "I disagree," you open yourself to further arguments. When you convey your opinion from a particular vantage point, you create space for dialogue. Any of these three phrases will help:

1. **"I see things differently."** There's a stark difference between "You're wrong" and "I see this differently." The first zooms in on the other person; the second zooms out on the situation.

2. **"I take another approach."** This reply refocuses the conversation on the goal you both want to achieve. It emphasizes collaboration over conflict. Even if you choose different routes, you reframe the conversation to the destination.

3. **"I tend to lean the opposite."** Say that, then state what you've normally done in similar situations. People are inclined to be more open to accepting your preferences than being abruptly attacked.

Note the sentence construction: *I* + present-tense verb. When in doubt about how to reply, let your first word be your breath, your second word be *I*, and your third word be a present-tense verb that leads into your conversational values and goals.

What do you fear may happen when you use these phrases the next time you need to disagree with someone?

___

Putting It All Together

When you have a plan in place *before* your ignition phase fires up, you'll be better equipped to handle insults, interruptions, bad apologies, and disagreements. You'll be able to stay calm and to speak the right words just when you need them. And the other person will realize that they're not dealing with the same person they're used to.

The pushover has become the immovable object. The quiet one has become the quiet but strong one. The mouse has become the lion.

Before you turn the page, let's do one last assessment. Review each question in this section that asked about your fears. Briefly list them all.

___

What similarities do you see?

_____

_____

_____

How will you commit to overcoming those fears in your next conversation with a difficult person?

_____

_____

_____

Boundaries

Chapter 9 in *The Next Conversation*

We were scrambling to get ready to head out the door to our kids' school program. My wife was throwing on her makeup, my daughter was combing her hair, and I was rushing to get my shoes on. My son, however, was operating on a totally different schedule. We were finally loading into the car when I realized he was still inside. Going through the house, I yelled out his name. I heard him from the playroom.

"Hey buddy, it's time to go. Let's go," I said with a little clap of my hands.

Without taking his eyes off his current LEGO project, he replied, "No, thank you though."

I pushed again, firmer. "Hey, I said let's go. Come on, please. We're going to be late."

"Sorry," he said sweetly. "Sorry, Dad, no thank you."

I couldn't help but laugh. "While I can appreciate the boundary, we gotta go!" I scooped him up, threw him over my shoulder, and ran toward the door while he screamed in excitement.

Children have no problem saying no bluntly and directly. They know their boundaries and will remind you of that fact every day. Just try to airplane that broccoli into their mouth at dinner. Or tell them it's bedtime. They know what they want, and they won't be shy about letting you know the same.

So why do we grow out of that?

Because we learn that our actions have consequences. And that other people have boundaries too. So you stay quiet for fear of punishment. Or you avoid conflict so everyone can get along. Or you stifle your wants and desires so that others can get what they want or desire.

Little by little, that clear, direct, fearless voice you had as a child disappears. As your boundaries decrease, it seems as if everyone else's increase. Soon enough, you may feel like you're a trespasser just for being you, apologizing for even taking up space.

Let's take the first, small step toward rightsizing your boundaries.

How to Say No (*TNC*, pp. 189–196)

When you have to say no to someone, you may be considering their response (their needs) over your own. When you excuse or justify your no, you're minding their boundary instead of your own.

You're also losing time and energy over what should be a simple back-and-forth.

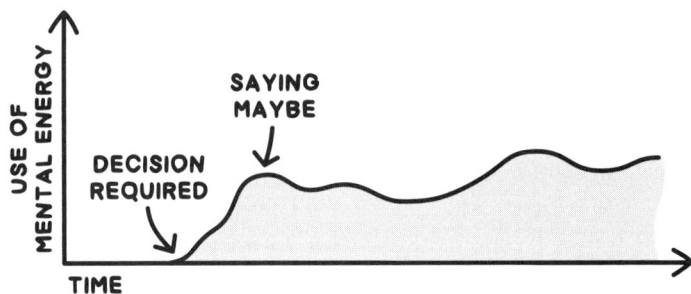

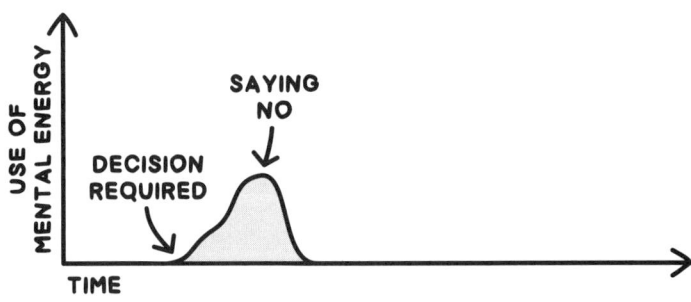

THE APPLICATION

The next time you need to turn someone down, do this:

1. **Say no.** "I can't." Be direct, because direct is kind.
2. **Show gratitude.** "I appreciate your asking me." Acknowledge the other person's gesture.
3. **Show kindness.** "I know it will be great." This curtails further questions and ends the conversation on a high note.

Note: refrain from using the word *but* anywhere in the sequence. Don't negate anything you've said.

Remember: no is a complete sentence.

On a scale of 1 (never) to 5 (always), how often do you struggle to say no to others? This could be in any setting, with any kind of person, in any kind of discussion, from the mundane to the major.

How do you typically say no? Are you short and direct? Do you have a go-to excuse?

_____

_____

How will using this strategy change how you approach the next person you need to say no to?

_____

_____

How to Build a Boundary (*TNC*, pp. 196–204)

For the toughest conversations, the most aggravating people, and the toxic relationships in your life, you need more than a no. You need a ready defense.

Forget about drawing a line. Establish a perimeter.

If saying no is closing a door, asserting a boundary is building a fortress with a moat.

Consider the many kinds of relationships you have and how your boundaries change from person to person. Describe your boundaries with each of these people in a few words. (Skip any that are irrelevant.) If visualization helps, you could describe the height and type of your boundary, e.g., a three-foot chain-link fence keeps them at bay; you can still hear and see them, but it isn't difficult to cross.

Spouse/partner/significant other: _____

Close family member: _____

Child: _____

Extended relative: _____

CEO/boss/manager: _____

Coworker: _____

Employee: _____

Close friend: _____

Acquaintance: _____

Stranger: _____

Other: _____

In the work you're about to do, you'll learn how to establish strong boundaries for any kind of relationship.

First, define your perimeter

Recall what's important to you. In the following box, list every value you hold dear. Examples include family, friends, career, well-being, health, self-respect, etc.

```
┌─────────────────────────────────────────────┐
│      EVERYTHING WITHIN THIS PERIMETER       │
│           MUST REMAIN PROTECTED             │
│                                             │
│                                             │
│                                             │
│                                             │
│                                             │
│                                             │
│                                             │
└─────────────────────────────────────────────┘
```

Values alone don't create a boundary. Your actions based on your values create a boundary. For example, establishing a boundary based on health means that when your best friend offers you the world's most delicious-looking donut, you say no (which you know how to do now). And because you've already set that boundary in your mind, the no should be assertive, effortless, and easy.

Your values don't turn into boundaries until you begin making intentional choices that put others on notice that *they are not allowed in*. You want them to see the moat you're digging.

Choose one of your values. Recall a recent conversation when you failed to establish a strong boundary based on that value. What do you think caused you to react that way?

_____

_____

_____

What could you have done differently to create a boundary based on that value?

_____

_____

_____

Next, know your manual

This internal manual is a list of automatic nos. If your life were a card game, it's the rules others have to follow to play the game. It's the words and actions that you won't allow past your moat.

Do you know what your manual says? While you may never have written them down, I bet you already know your automatic nos. Commit them to paper here, and then commit to abiding by them when you most need them. Here are a few examples, but spend some thoughtful time writing down five to ten of your own. You may even want to come back to this question as new manual entries come to mind during your day.

- "I don't respond to disrespect."

- "I will not allow others to tell me or to decide how I feel."
- "I don't engage in conversation when I'm not ready."

- _____
- _____
- _____
- _____
- _____
- _____
- _____
- _____
- _____
- _____

Here's how this can play out in real life. If an ignited friend is yelling at you, you may be tempted to scream back, "Stop yelling at me!" But when you pause and remember to hand them your manual, your reply becomes "I don't respond to that volume." That's a short, strong, calm statement that cools the conversation and establishes a boundary.

The first response admits *I have no control*.

The second response states *I am in control*.

Who do you want to be?

Lastly, enforce your boundary

At this point, you have to tell the other person what they've run into *and* that they're not going any further.

1. **Begin with the boundary.** Start with *I*, state your boundary, then say nothing, e.g., "I don't accept how you're treating me." If the other person relents and shows respect for your boundary, well done. If they push, go to step two.

2. **Add the consequence.** Tell them what will happen if they keep crossing your boundary, e.g., "If you continue to . . . I'm going to . . ." Together, these two steps look like this: "I don't accept how you're treating me. If you continue to treat me this way, I'm going to end the conversation." This table offers more examples.

If they . . .	Then you . . .	And the consequence is . . .
Go off topic	Re-center the conversation: "I came here to talk about this topic."	"If you continue to go off topic, I will need to continue the conversation another time."
Attack your character	Respond with: "I don't respond to disrespect."	"If you continue to treat me this way, I am going to end the conversation."
Raise past issues	Stand your ground: "I am not going there with you."	"If you continue to bring up the past, I will not be able to engage with you to find a solution."

If they relent, your job is done. If not, go to the last—and most difficult—step.

3. **Follow through.** Asserting yourself is telling the other person what you're going to do, then doing it. If you say "I'm going to end the conversation" and they continue pressing into your boundary and you *don't* end the conversation, you've weakened your position. You've lowered your drawbridge. You've relented to their boundary. Plus, when you say something that you know you'll have to follow through on, you'll say it with conviction.

Have you given a consequence to someone and then didn't follow through? What happened in that situation?

_____

_____

_____

_____

_____

How did it affect the relationship, both in the short term and the long term?

_____

_____

_____

Review your manual. Add consequences to each item.

_____

_____

_____

Review your consequences. Will you really follow through on each of them? Even with the people closest to you?

_____

_____

How will you promise yourself that you'll follow through?

_____

_____

_____

What do you fear about setting new boundaries? It may also help to think about how new boundaries will affect your many kinds of relationships, e.g., spouse, friends, coworkers, etc.

___

___

___

How Setting Boundaries Changes Your Relationships
(*TNC*, pp. 204–205)

To be honest, it can be fearful to set new boundaries. Some won't like it. Some will hate it. Boundaries have a way of sifting out those who are with you not because of who you are but because of what they need you to be.

When you move your boundaries, others can feel like you've reoriented their universe without their permission. You're not the *you* they thought you were—or want you to be. Their discomfort over your boundary is not a sign that it's wrong; it's a sign that it's working.

Establishing new boundaries will test some of your relationships. Give others grace as you make the change. Keep your eyes and ears open to see who's in your corner, the ones who love you for who you are and not for what you can give them or do for them.

Start small. Build one new boundary soon. Feel the confidence of the words you say and the consequences you may need to demand. Follow through. See how it affects your relationships. Better still, see how it affects you. Confidence builds upon confidence.

What do you hope new boundaries will accomplish for you?

___

___

___

Whom in your life do you need to have some difficult, boundary-setting conversations with? Which manual entries might apply? Figure out now what you'd like to say then. Write their names below. Then write your boundary and consequence statements. And be sure to commit to yourself that you'll follow through by doing what you say you're going to do.

___

___

___

___

___

___

___

THE APPLICATION

Rule 2 Review

Fill in the following blanks. On your first pass, try to fill in what you remember. On your second pass, go back through the chapters and fill in any words you may have missed. Circle any of the steps that you want to start using today in your life and conversations.

Rule 2: Say it with _____.

- Find your _____.
  - Every _____ matters.
  - _____ it to yourself.
  - Express your needs _____.
  - _____ when it matters.
  - Say _____.
  - Remove _____ words.
  - Never _____.
  - Cut the _____.
  - When in doubt, fall back on _____.
  - Say "I'm _____."
  - Mind your _____.

- Stand your ground with _____
  _____.

  - When they insult or offend:

    * Give it a _____.

    * Slowly _____ what they said.

    * Keep _____ out.

  - When they belittle, patronize, or condescend:

    * Make them _____
      _____.

    * Ask a question of _____.

    * Reply with _____.

  - When they're rude or dismissive:

    * Give it a _____.

    * Ask a question of _____.

    * W_____.

  - The five types of bad apologies are:

    * The no-e_____ apology

    * The no-a_____ apology

    * The e_____ apology

- * The t_____ apology
- * The j_____ apology

- When they interrupt you:
  - * Let the other person _____ you.
  - * Use their _____.
  - * _____ the behavior.

- How to disagree better:
  - * Apply the _____ _____ _____ filter.
  - * Use your _____ point.

- Establish your _____.
  - How to say no:
    - * Say _____.
    - * Show g_____.
    - * Show k_____.
  - How to build a boundary:
    - * Define your _____.

* Know your _____.

* _____ your boundary.

    1. _____ with the boundary.

    2. Add the _____.

    3. _____ through.

THE APPLICATION

Extra note space:

RULE 3

Say It to Connect

"Can you believe what she wrote?!" my client exclaimed, shoving her phone's screen in my face.

Moving my head away to read, I saw a text: "Sure, if that's what you think."

"Is this the text you've been so upset about?" I asked calmly.

"I mean, she's so selfish, right? She could've said 'Sounds good,' but no, she sent that just to spite me," she replied, her voice tightening with frustration.

Taking a pause, I started to help her unravel the knot. "Let's look at this from a thousand-foot view," I said. "If you ignore the tone you think you hear, what's something you can learn from her reply? And what's something you're trying to prove?"

Her expression shifted as the question sunk in. She glanced down, her face softening. "I'm learning that . . . I should just call her, huh."

"You're learning that you should call her," I echoed, nodding gently.

A few minutes later, she dialed her friend. As they talked, her posture changed—relaxed, lighter. Turns out, the tone behind the text wasn't critical or spiteful at all. It was positive, even supportive. Far from the narrative my client had built in her mind.

She'd almost let an assumption ruin her opportunity for connection.

How often do you make the same mistake?

Let's say you've mastered the first two steps of my framework. You can say it with control and you can say it with confidence. You feel stronger within, and the other people in your life can't help but notice your newfound assertiveness. But if that's as far as you get, or if that's all you think you need to improve your next conversation, you're going to miss out on an essential strategy that seeks the health of the relationship: how to say it *to connect*.

In this section, we're going to discuss how to:

- Frame a conversation

- Prevent defensiveness

- Have difficult conversations

In each case, the goal is connection. Remember: Never win an argument. Don't see the other person as the problem. See the problem as the problem. Then work together to unravel it.

You can be in control and confident, but without seeking to connect, you'll just be right—and lonely.

Frames

Chapter 10 in *The Next Conversation*

Some conversations can feel like going to the grocery store with a toddler. They grab anything that looks enticing. They dart up and down the aisles. There's no guessing what they'll do next. When your conversations feel aimless and chaotic, you wonder, *What's the point?* You throw out your goal in favor of just surviving the moment.

The conversation needs to be placed in the shopping cart. This is what I mean by setting a conversational frame. You're strapping down your discussion so you both can achieve a goal.

When you limit the pathways the conversation can take, you're helping yourself and the other person by making it easier to connect and find each other in the conversation.

By framing your conversations, you will:

- Narrow the focus
- Get both parties on the same page
- Set expectations for what's off topic
- Corral wandering topics

When you don't frame a conversation, here's what can happen:

- The conversation drags on and on and on.

- Misinterpretation, confusion, or misunderstanding (by either party) has a longer time to reveal itself.

- The conversation ends and you feel as if nothing was accomplished or, worse, damage was done.

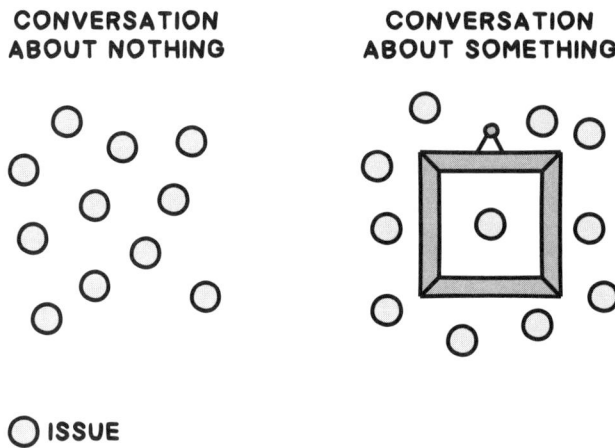

How have you experienced the lack of framing in a recent conversation? (Either party could have been the culprit.)

_____

_____

What words or actions tipped you off that the conversation didn't have a goal?

_____

_____

How did you feel when the conversation ended?

_____

_____

_____

One clear sign that you've failed to use a conversational frame is hearing the other person ask things like "What's your point?" or "What are you wanting me to do?" (when you don't want them to do anything). That means your words meandered too much for the other person to understand your expectations and desires. Unclear parameters leave the other person playing the detective, which can frustrate them or induce anxiety. Remove their fear of the unknown by clearly framing what you want to discuss.

How to Frame a Conversation (*TNC*, pp. 215–219)

You don't need to frame *every* conversation. But for the moments when you need to be intentional, when you want to come away from a conversation with clear next steps for everyone involved, try setting a frame.

1. **Set a direction.** Do this at the beginning of the conversation. Don't wait until you think it's necessary. If you want the conversation to have a destination, set the direction before anyone's engines have warmed up. Point them where you want to go. Begin with phrases like "I want to . . ." or "I'd like to . . ." or "I need to . . ." Then include your conversational values and goals. Altogether, that could look like this:

- "I'd like to talk with you about a subject personal to me."

- "I need to discuss our plans for next week."

- "I want to talk about what you said the other day."

2. **Call your shot.** You've set the direction. Now set the destination. How do you want the conversation to end? How do you want to feel? Be specific. The most helpful words I've found are how I'd finish the phrase "And by the end of it . . ." That could look like this:

    - "[And by the end of it,] I want to be heard without your feeling like you need to fix it."

    - "[And by the end of it,] I want you to know that I still love you and want to be together."

3. **Get their commitment.** Plainly ask if they will agree to the direction and destination. If you're in the driver's seat, will they get into the car with you? This can take the form of saying:

    - "Can we agree to that?"

    - "Is that doable for you?"

    - "That sound good to you?"

Now you're going to put all of that together in a few role-playing exercises. Imagine you're grabbing coffee with a close friend. You recently learned that they were gossiping about you. You don't know what was said, and you're not 100 percent sure that the friend said anything at all. But you know you need to bring it up. You won't be able to talk to them normally until you do. Using the framing techniques you've learned, what will you say?

THE APPLICATION

1. Set a direction: _____
2. Call your shot: _____
3. Get their commitment: _____
4. Put it all together: _____
   _____
   _____

Imagine you're talking with your manager. You're overdue for a raise. You know this because a few of your less-experienced coworkers have recently gotten raises. How will you frame that conversation?

1. Set a direction: _____
2. Call your shot: _____
3. Get their commitment: _____
4. Put it all together: _____
   _____
   _____

Imagine you're talking with your spouse or significant other about your combined budget. (If there's any conversation that can run wild like a toddler, it's a budget conversation.) You're sticking to what you've agreed to, but your partner is overspending. No consequences have struck the two of you yet, but you know it's only a matter of time. How will you frame that conversation?

1. Set a direction: _____
2. Call your shot: _____

3. Get their commitment: _____

4. Put it all together: _____
   _____
   _____

Finally, let's make this less hypothetical. What's the difficult conversation you've been putting off?

_____

_____

_____

Maybe you've been postponing it because the subject seems too large. There are too many options, too many paths for the conversation to take. But commit to taking the first step toward connection by choosing one small, specific area to focus on.

What's the one issue or topic you can discuss with that person?

_____

_____

How will you frame that conversation?

1. Set a direction: _____

2. Call your shot: _____

3. Get their commitment: _____

4. Put it all together: _____

_____

_____

Remember: one frame, one conversation.

When you have a goal, don't get overconfident and shoot for more. With just one frame per conversation, every word becomes more intentional. Plus, a focused conversation is often a more meaningful conversation, where each person has the time and space to offer thoughtful, measured, rational contributions.

Still, even your best efforts to frame an important conversation can fall short. When a talk wanders out of your frame, here's what you can do to get the conversation back on course.

How to Nudge a Conversation Back into View
(*TNC*, pp. 220–223)

When either person begins chasing a rabbit, use the keyword of your goal. For example, if you're discussing the budget, say *budget* at some point. You can also be blunt and say, "We're getting off track."

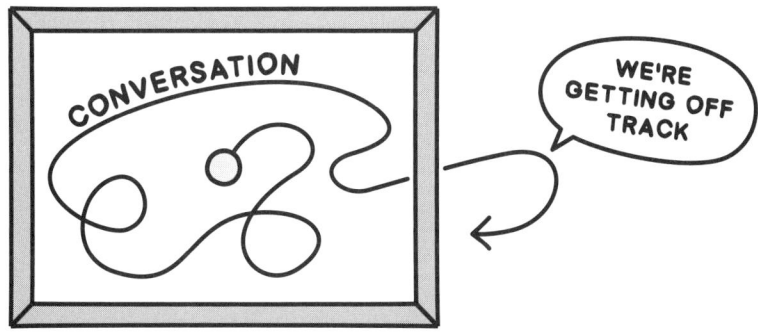

Those are the easy nudges. What about when the conversation needs a shove?

This is particularly necessary in difficult conversations when the other person changes the topic because they don't want to talk about the issue you've framed. They may do this on purpose or subconsciously. Either way, they've altered the destination. They've taken the driver's seat. And you're presented with a choice whether to ride along or take back the wheel.

In my opinion, the worst kind of deflection is the "you too" comeback: "Oh really? You did the same thing to me last year." They feel the heat of the spotlight and force it back on you. Don't let their attack ignite you. Acknowledge what they said and then calmly refocus the conversation on the initial topic. Here's how that sounds.

- "I hear your point. I need to finish what we started. And if needed, I'm willing to come back and address that comment."

- "I agree that's worth talking about too. Let's focus on one issue at a time."

In the instances when you're the one to go outside the frame, try this:

1. Apologize for what you said that derailed the conversation. "I'm sorry I raised my voice."
2. Speak words that convey distance from the goal. "That wasn't fair."
3. Pick up where you left off. "Here's what I was trying to say."

What people in your life tend to derail your conversations? What do they say or do that suddenly changes the topic?

_____

_____

THE APPLICATION

_____

_____

_____

Why do you think they do that?

_____

_____

_____

_____

The next time they derail you, how will you nudge the conversation back into view? Write down what you could say.

_____

_____

_____

_____

Defensiveness

Chapter 11 in *The Next Conversation*

There is little that's more costly to your next conversation than the price of defensiveness. When walls go up, relational health goes down. The longer a person's defensive stance stays firm, the harder it becomes to find resolution. Distance grows. The wall gets taller. And your motivation to see the relationship get healthy wanes.

To be blunt, the cost of defensiveness could be the death of a relationship.

Think about the ways defensiveness shows up in your relationships. Check the ways that you display defensiveness.

- ☐ Using sarcasm
- ☐ Giving the silent treatment
- ☐ Laughing off serious topics
- ☐ Interrupting others
- ☐ Leaving the conversation
- ☐ Raising your voice
- ☐ Verbally attacking others
- ☐ Dismissing others' views
- ☐ Making generalizations
- ☐ Deflecting by bringing up past grievances
- ☐ Playing the victim
- ☐ Denying the issue at hand
- ☐ Blaming the other person
- ☐ Ignoring their boundaries
- ☐ Using passive-aggressive behavior or words
- ☐ Other: _____

Where did you learn these defensive measures? Take some time to consider how these may have been modeled for you while you were growing up. Who modeled it? What did it look like or sound like?

_____

_____

_____

_____

Which defensive measure seems to be the most problematic for you to control?

_____

_____

_____

Which defensive measure frustrates you the most when someone else deploys it? Why?

_____

_____

_____

_____

Now check the phrases you've said in the past.

- ☐ "Yeah, but you didn't even . . ."
- ☐ "You can't actually be serious!"
- ☐ "You're such an idiot."
- ☐ "You don't even care."
- ☐ "What about the time that you . . ."
- ☐ "You never listen to me."
- ☐ "You always do this!"
- ☐ "You don't know what really happened."
- ☐ "You don't know what I've been through."

What do your common defensive phrases say about your common defensive posture? Put another way, what similarities do you see between the defensive measures you checked and the defensive phrases you checked?

_____

_____

_____

_____

_____

Do you believe that it's possible *not* to become defensive, even in your most difficult conversations? Why or why not?

_____

_____

_____

Why Defensiveness Breaks Connection (*TNC*, pp. 228–236)

The defensive phrases have one word in common: *you*. When your defensiveness gets ignited, an accusatory *you* is often the first word that your fight-or-flight response reaches for. *You* is the first brick in the wall you're building.

When your ignition phase is at its peak, do you find yourself prone to defensiveness? If so, why do you believe that's the case?

_____

_____

_____

Most often, we build walls due to cognitive dissonance. What the other person has said or done clashes with your existing beliefs or expectations. You don't want to listen because you're uncomfortable. If you don't remove yourself from the discomfort (flight), you will likely dig your heels in deeper (fight). The wall goes up to protect the part of you that feels under attack. And the more arrows they launch, the larger the artillery you want to launch in return.

Describe the last time you dug in your heels. What did it look like? Sound like? How did you feel in that moment?

_____

_____

_____

What was the immediate result?

_____

_____

_____

How is that relationship today?

_____

_____

_____

When you put up walls, you prevent others from understanding you and you shut yourself off from understanding them. The deeper problem is that you accept the consequences of the latter but dismiss the consequences of the former. Put another way, you lower all expectations of yourself while maintaining your same expectations of the other person.

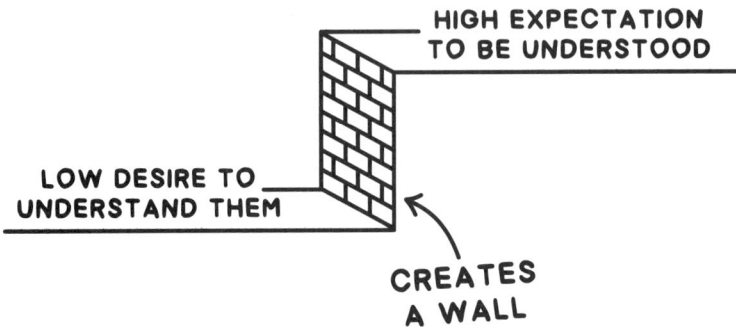

You can know you're doing this when, in the heat of an argument, you think, *Well, they should know how I feel* or *They should know what I'm thinking.* Unless they've scaled the wall you've built, they have no idea what you're feeling or thinking. In shutting them out, you've shut out your voice too.

You can also know you're being unreasonably defensive when you let yourself off the hook with rational excuses but make up reasons for why other people are being difficult. Psychologists call this the fundamental attribution error, where we tend to overemphasize personality-based explanations and underemphasize external situational factors. For example, if a coworker dashes by you without saying hi, you may be annoyed that you weren't acknowledged. You may worry that you've upset them. But the truth is that your coworker was running late for an important meeting.

In what situation have you most recently committed a fundamental attribution error?

_____

_____

_____

THE APPLICATION

How did you feel when you learned the truth?

_____

_____

What will you commit to do in order to give others the benefit of the doubt?

_____

_____

Let's shift perspectives. When your wall is up, just hearing the word *you* coming from the other person can be received as a direct attack, even when it's not intended that way. Because the guards around your castle are on high alert, any perceived threat is dealt with as an actual threat.

A vicious cycle begins:

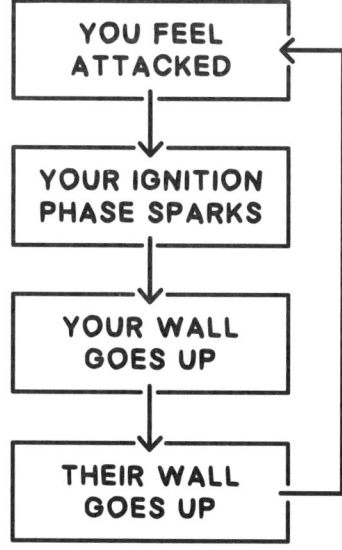

In the worst instances, the goal becomes who can build the tallest, strongest wall. But there are better ways to invest the limited amount of time you have on Earth.

How to Stop Your Defensiveness (*TNC*, pp. 236–239)

How often you take things personally is a direct reflection of how much grace you give other people. The advice we give our children applies to us as well: What if the shoe was on the other foot? Are you giving as much grace as you would like to be given?

Being willing to see beyond yourself will transform how you interact with the world. Remember: the person you see is not the person you're talking to. Just like you, they contain multitudes. So much is going on in their life that you don't know about, all of which is likely a greater contributor to your argument than what you think is at play. Consider how many times you've been in an argument and wished, *If only they knew about . . .*

Your defensiveness seeks to protect you when you believe the other person thinks you're wrong or flawed. This hits every psychological trigger discussed in chapter four of *The Next Conversation*.

- **Social evaluation:** If I'm wrong, will I be humiliated? Will they reject me?

- **Personal identity:** If I'm wrong, do I still matter? Am I defective?

- **Loss:** If I'm wrong, will they walk away? Will I lose my reputation?

Rank these triggers in the order of how quickly they make you defensive, with 1 being the issue that can immediately ignite you. For each trigger, write a line or two about how that looks or sounds. (To remind yourself of these definitions, see chapter four of *The Next Conversation*.)

___ Social evaluation

_____

_____

___ Personal identity

_____

_____

___ Loss

_____

_____

When you feel even the slightest pressure increase on any of your triggers, try this to prevent your defensiveness from getting a foothold in your mind and body.

1. **Catch yourself.** Take nine seconds to do a conversational breath. Remember: control yourself, control the moment, control the pace. Plus, slow breathing tells your body that you're not facing a real threat.

2. **Let their words fall.** As you're paused, imagine their words falling to the ground. Consider whether it's worth your time to pick them up. You don't have to attend every argument you're invited to.

3. **Get curious.** Instead of being a defense attorney, be a cold-case investigator. Try to figure out where their issue is coming from or what's driving them to say what they're saying. Let the heat dissipate so your reply is calm and cool.

Here's another strategy (and one that's not in *The Next Conversation*): don't interrupt. When you do that, you're telling the other person that what you have to say is far more important than what they have to say. Rather, let them get it all out. How could you pour new thoughts into a glass that's already full? Just like you, they've been thinking all day about what they want to say to you. So let them pour it all out.

When you think they're done, ask, "Anything else?" They'll finish their pour or they'll be done. Then you can address the point.

Also, don't follow up with "Yeah, but . . ." or "Okay, but . . ." Leave your *but* out of it. Just say, "Okay. I hear you. I understand." Then address the issue.

Now you've told your defensiveness to stand down. Your mind and body realize they're not under actual attack. You can approach the conversation with more openness and more levelheadedness—and with a chosen goal to connect with the other person.

But here's the truth of what can still happen: in your silence, they've added more bricks to their wall. If the first word you lob over that wall is *you*, well, you've restarted the cycle of defensiveness. One simple change can stop that.

How to Prevent Their Defensiveness (*TNC*, pp. 239–242)

Instead of *you*, begin with *I*. *You* is a live grenade. *I* is a bomb squad defusing the situation. *You* points a finger. *I* takes responsibility. *You* triggers. *I* connects.

For example, instead of accusing someone with "*You're* always looking at your phone," try "I enjoy sharing time together without our screens."

THE APPLICATION

Now it's your turn. Transform each of the following *you* accusations into positive, connecting statements that begin with *I*.

- "You don't appreciate me."
    - "I _____."

- "You can't speak to me that way."
    - "I _____."

- "You think you're always right."
    - "I _____."

- "You're not listening to me."
    - "I _____."

- "You never want to do what I want to do."
    - "I _____."

Notice how the simple shift to yourself takes the focus off the other person (preventing their defensiveness) while also making you sound more assertive.

There's another word choice decision you can make early on in the conversation to accomplish the same thing. When you're tempted to ask *why*, use *what*, *when*, or *how* instead.

Why is this the case? Because *why* implies wrongdoing, blame, or judgment. *Why* questions autonomy. Think of the last time someone asked you, "Why did you say that?" How did you react?

Here's an example: instead of asking "*Why* didn't you take the trash out?" try "*When* are you planning on taking out the trash?"

Now it's your turn. Rephrase these statements to be less accusatory.

- "Why'd you do it like that?"

    – "_____?"

- "Why can't you just relax?"

    – "_____?"

- "Why do you think you're right?"

    – "_____?"

- "Why are we going this way?"

    – "_____?"

- "Why are you talking to me like that?"

    – "_____?"

You're taking the spotlight off the person and placing it on the problem.

Here's one last tip that can prevent even the most experienced wall builders from getting defensive: acknowledge them first.

Consider how frustrating it is when you're not heard. Extend the grace you desire to others. Make sure that *they're* heard by validating their feelings or perspective before presenting your own. This doesn't mean you have to agree with what they say. But you do have to agree that their perspective has as much value as yours. Here are three ways to do that.

1. **Tell them what you agree with.** Seek common ground, even if that patch of land is just a square foot. Maybe the only agreement you can make is "I agree this topic is worth discussing." That still works.

2. **Tell them what you've learned.** Admitting that the other person has taught you something will make the other person stand a little bit taller. You're also giving evidence that you're listening. You can be specific about the lesson you've been taught, or you can say something general like "I've learned that this subject is very important to you."

3. **Tell them that they're helpful.** Acknowledging helpfulness often leads to the other person remaining more open and forthcoming. They want to continue to be helpful, and this supports the both of you focusing on the problem and not on each other. This can be as simple as saying "That's helpful to know."

When you feel someone else getting defensive, change your words from those that put up walls to those that break them down. Don't confront. Connect.

What will you commit to do the next time you feel your defensiveness rising?

_____

_____

And what will you commit to do the next time you see someone else's walls go up?

_____

_____

Difficult Conversations

Chapter 12 in *The Next Conversation*

If you've worked section by section to get here, I'm giving you a standing ovation. Thoughtfully considering how you're going to approach your next conversation when you're not in the heat of an argument should help you maintain your cool. I promise you: the work you've done will pay off in your relationships.

If you've skipped to this section because this is the help you need most, let me encourage you. By choosing to pick up this workbook, you've accepted the challenge to break the cycle of winning arguments. You'd rather mend relationships than build walls. You'd rather connect than seek conflict. And you're ready to stand up for yourself, from the most mundane requests to the most difficult conversations.

But one word of warning if you've skipped to here: start with part one. To handle difficult conversations most effectively, you need to know how to control your emotions and hone your assertive voice. Without those tools, you won't be able to say it with control, say it with confidence, and, most importantly, say it to connect.

Good? Good. Now let's talk about the hard stuff.

Write the name of the person with whom you've been putting off a difficult conversation. Next to their name, write why you've been putting it off.

What fears lie behind your hesitation?

_____

_____

_____

_____

Keep this person in mind as you work through the following steps.

The Three Rules to Approaching Difficult Conversations
(*TNC*, pp. 247–259)

If the conversation you've been putting off involves firing someone, breaking up, discussing finances, or any of the hundreds of issues that make conversations difficult, I feel for you. None of us actively seeks hard conversations. Why would we voluntarily light our ignition phase?

But we're all human. Arguments, misunderstandings, and disagreements happen. Let's not make them any harder than they have to be.

A difficult conversation becomes more difficult for two reasons:

1. You don't know where you're going.
2. You don't know how to get there.

If you don't believe me, think about how many times you've played out a difficult conversation in your head versus how often the real-life conversation plays out that way.

Recall the last time you thought you knew how a hard conversation was going to go. What did you think (or hope) would happen?

_____

_____

What actually happened?

_____

_____

Did any of your assumptions hold true?

_____

_____

If so, what was the noticeable turning point in your actual conversation? In other words, where did reality diverge from your expectations?

_____

_____

If you can't gauge how another person will respond, can you do anything worthwhile to prepare for a difficult conversation? Is it possible to figure out your destination and your route while still seeking connection more than victory?

The best time to remove the *difficult* from a difficult conversation is before it even starts. Approach is everything.

1. Set aside real, undistracted time

If you're going to have a difficult conversation, remove the external factors that make it more difficult. This includes variables like where and when the conversation takes place, as well as the possibility for interruptions. For example:

- Find a private, comfortable setting—somewhere that the other person finds agreeable.

- If you know that the other person is more focused at a particular time of the day, schedule your talk during that time frame.

- As you silence your phone, ask them to do the same. Say, "This is an important conversation and I'd like to ensure no distractions."

Now think about the person you need to have a difficult conversation with. List the ways you can remove distracting external factors.

- The setting should be _____.

- The timing should be _____.

- The interruptions I can proactively remove include _____ _____.

- Other variables I should consider are _____ _____ _____.

THE APPLICATION

The timing of hard conversations is crucial. No one wants a bomb dropped on them without warning. Don't do unto others what you don't want done unto you. Don't demand a difficult conversation *now*. Rather, set an assigned time in the future to have the discussion. For example, you could say:

- "When would be a good time Friday morning to go over . . . ?"
- "Do you have capacity to talk about Monday's meeting agenda this afternoon?"
- "Do you have the bandwidth to talk about the kids' schedule for tomorrow once they go down for bed?"

I like to use the words *capacity* and *bandwidth* to show respect for the other person's time *and* their mental or emotional load. Sure, they may be available to talk at the time you've said, but what if it's right after a double shift?

Suggest a narrow time frame or a particular time of day in the future. This benefits both people by giving them time to prepare. Remember, the fewer choices you give, the easier it becomes for people to decide.

In the following list, check the best ways to ask for a person's time.

- ☐ "When is a good time next week?"
- ☐ "Are you available Thursday night to talk?"
- ☐ "Got a second?"
- ☐ "I need to talk to you."
- ☐ "Could we chat in thirty minutes?"
- ☐ "When are you free later?"
- ☐ "Quick question."
- ☐ "We should talk. You free on Monday at one p.m. for maybe an hour?"

The answers are the phrases that specify a time.

Note the last answer: "for maybe an hour." The best way to ask for someone's time to have a difficult conversation includes a time frame. Show the other person that the length of the conversation respects the topic. Serious, sensitive, or negative topics all need more time. This allows both parties to offer their full focus. It also gives you time to include intentional pauses, to keep the conversation within your frame, and to do everything else you've learned in this workbook.

How will you ask your difficult-conversation person about when they can meet with you?

___

How soon will you say that to this person?

___

If they deny your request, what will you say?

___

2. Drop the pleasantries

"How's your day been?"

"Susie's really growing up fast."

"I can't believe this weather."

I get it. I really do. You mean well. But small talk before hard conversations serves no one. Putting off the inevitable is the worst thing you can do. People know. When the shoe is on the other foot—when you're the one about to receive bad news, for instance—you know. You can feel it, hear it, see it. Something's just off. You'd rather the person just get to the point, pull off the Band-Aid, and tell you the truth of the matter.

So offer others the same grace and respect.

Don't start with pleasantries. Be direct.

The simplest way is the most direct. Say, "This is going to be a difficult conversation." For bad news, you could say, "I've got bad news." For sensitive topics, you could say, "This isn't going to be easy to talk about." Your goal is to quickly and clearly state the nature of the conversation you want to have. It's framing the conversation so the other person knows what to expect. By being direct up-front, you calm their rising ignition phase.

Also, be sure to pause after saying "This is going to be difficult." They know they're about to hear something they don't want to hear or didn't expect to hear. So let the other person's mind and body catch up to what you just said. You'll probably even notice audible or visual cues—a deep breath or a shift in posture—that lets you know they're ready. Then, just as clearly, quickly, and boldly, tell them what you need to tell them, e.g., "I need to let you go."

Think about when you're the one in the hot seat. Let's say your boss calls you in. You know something's up, but they start with "How was your weekend?" You both know that's not the true discussion. Even as you answer the pleasantries (because you're nice and you respect your boss), you're thinking, *What's this really about?* You fidget and worry until your boss says, "Well, I've called you in because . . ." And in that moment, you relax. *Finally*, you think. Even if the news is bad, at least you're no longer wondering why you're there.

What small-talk phrases or topics most annoy you?

Describe the last time you were on the receiving end of bad news. Did the other person act nice before delivering the gut punch? What did they say or do? How did you respond?

_____

_____

_____

Clarity is kind. It removes the ambiguity and anxiety that can cloud difficult conversations, allowing both of you to connect to the reality of the situation.

In the following list, check the better ways to start hard conversations.

☐ "This isn't going to be fun for either of us."

☐ "Good lunch?"

☐ "I have something uncomfortable to share."

☐ "You're not going to like what I have to say."

☐ "So, how are you?"

☐ "This might come as a shock to you."

☐ "What have you been up to lately?"

☐ "I'm really disappointed in you."

☐ "Thank you for making time to talk with me."

☐ "We need to talk about your performance."

Note: it's okay to thank the other person for meeting with you. Just be sure that the phrase that follows lets them know it will be a hard conversation.

What pleasantries are you guilty of using with others?

_____

_____

_____

Describe the last time you had to deliver bad news. How did you approach it? Once the conversation started, how long did it take you to get to the point of your conversation?

_____

_____

_____

What will you commit to do the next time you have to deliver bad news?

_____

_____

_____

3. Begin with your end

In difficult conversations, lead with your takeaway. I like to think of it as if I'm giving a presentation. When I start, I show the last slide first, the one titled "In Conclusion."

This prevents you from hedging your confidence or wandering away from your goal. It also prevents the other person's mind from wandering. It's clear and direct, the keywords you should keep in mind for any hard conversation.

DO THIS

YOUR POINT
[text]

NOT THIS

[text]
YOUR POINT

This strategy helps in all kinds of situations, but let's look at text messages—especially the ones where you feel the need to explain yourself. For example, rather than listing every reason you can't attend an event you've been invited to, cut everything *before* your actual answer. A simple "I can't make it tonight. Thanks for the invite. Have fun!" is clear and kind. Plus, the more words you have to use, the more you sound like you're lying.

In the following scenarios, cross out what's unnecessary.

- **At home:** "You overspent on groceries this week. And you want to go to a restaurant tonight? I just . . . I really would like us to try to rein in this spending. We need to talk about our budget. If we're not careful, we could be in some hurt pretty soon."

- **At work:** "We saw some errors in your latest report. I know you've been working long hours these last few weeks, but that can't be an excuse for poor work. You and I both know that our company can't afford these kinds of mistakes, especially if they keep happening. We're going to put you on a performance improvement plan beginning immediately."

- **With a friend:** "I almost cancelled on you today. I know I was the one to invite you. But I'm just not feeling great today, to be honest. I guess I'm just tired. Actually, you know what, on second thought, there is something that's been bothering me. Can we talk about the fact that I feel like I'm the one carrying this friendship? Like, I'm always the one doing the inviting."

In each of those scenarios, you can still say every sentence—just lead with the takeaway. In the same way that dropping pleasantries lets a person relax, beginning with your end lets a person immediately know what's expected. They see the destination long before you arrive. And that sets them at ease, even if what they're hearing might be hard to hear.

Do you struggle with being up-front in hard conversations? If so, why? What do you fear the other person will think about you if you're direct? Or how are you trying to make yourself feel by not being direct?

_____

_____

_____

If you're already a direct person, what effect has your bluntness had on other people (and particularly in hard conversations)? Do you need to lean into your bluntness or soften it in some way? In other words, what could you do differently to ensure that your clarity is kind?

_____

_____

_____

What It Means to Be a Safe Space (*TNC*, pp. 259–263)

Your reaction to someone else's coming to you with a difficult conversation will determine whether they ever come to you again. Creating space for difficult conversations begins with how you first receive the information. The next time someone comes to you with bad news or a sensitive topic, try these phrases.

- "I'm glad you came to me with this."
- "Thank you for telling me."
- "I appreciate your perspective."

Difficult conversations, despite the label, are your greatest opportunity to connect to another person. But the following commonly used replies in hard conversations will sever that connection.

- "I know what you're going through."
- "I had a hard day too."
- "Something like that happened to me once."

THE APPLICATION

You believe you're offering empathy, but what you're really doing is throwing a hook around the other person, yanking them off center stage, and then sliding into the spotlight. What used to be *we* is now just *me*.

If the other person came to you, this is the other person's conversation to drive. Be a kind passenger. Rather than taking the wheel by talking about yourself, lean back, relax, and get inquisitive.

1. **Ask one follow-up question.** It can be as simple as "How did that make you feel?" or "What do you think about that?"

2. **Ask permission.** Sometimes your life experiences are helpful to share, but get their buy-in first. Ask, "Do you mind if I share something with you?" Because you've expressed interest in step one, they'll likely say yes.

3. **Don't preach.** Instead of telling them what they should do or what you would do, ask, "Can I tell you what I've learned?" If you've followed these steps in order, they should be open to hearing your take.

The goal is to be a safe place for them to have hard conversations. Remember: the deeper the relationship you want to have with someone, the deeper the tolerance you must have for difficult conversations.

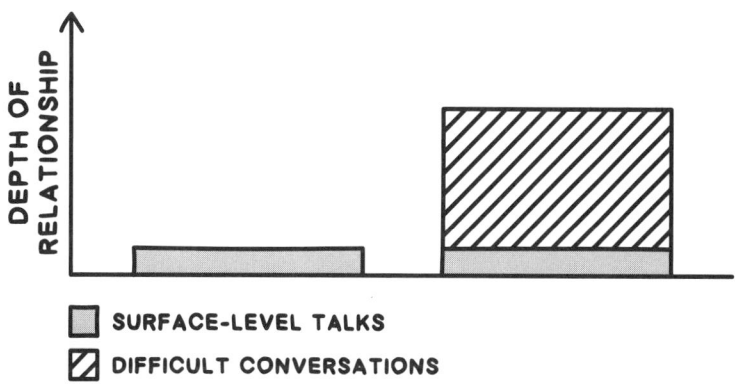

Do you often fight the urge to share "yeah, me too" experiences? What are the benefits to sharing your story? What are the drawbacks?

_____

_____

_____

The next time someone comes to you with a difficult conversation, what do you commit to say and do so that you can be a safe place for them?

_____

_____

_____

THE APPLICATION

Rule 3 Review

Fill in the following blanks. On your first pass, try to fill in what you remember. On your second pass, go back through the sections and fill in any words you may have missed. Circle any of the steps that you want to start using today in your life and conversations.

Rule 3: Say it to _____.

- How to frame a conversation:

    - Set a _____.

    - Call your _____.

    - Get their _____.

- How to stop your defensiveness:

    - _____ yourself.

    - Let their words _____.

    - Get _____.

- How to prevent their defensiveness:

    - Instead of _____, begin with _____.

    - Don't ask _____. Instead, ask _____, _____, or _____.

- _____ them first.

  * Tell them what you _____ with.

  * Tell them what you've _____.

  * Tell them that they're _____.

- How to have difficult conversations:

  - Set aside _____, _____ time.

  - Drop the _____.

  - _____ with your _____.

  - Be a _____.

THE APPLICATION

Extra note space:

ANSWER KEY

Rule 1 Review

Rule 1: Say it with control.

- Control yourself.
  - The two phases of every argument are ignition and cooling.
  - Psychological triggers arrive in three ways:
    * Social evaluation triggers
    * Personal identity triggers
    * Loss triggers
- Control the moment.
  - Your first word is your breath.
  - Your first thought is a quick scan.
  - Your first conversation is a small talk.
- Control the pace.
  - Short pauses are reading glasses.

- Long pauses are <u>mirrors</u>.
- There's <u>power</u> in the pause.

Rule 2 Review

Rule 2: Say it with <u>confidence</u>.

- Find your <u>assertive</u> <u>voice</u>.
    - Every <u>word</u> matters.
    - <u>Prove</u> it to yourself.
    - Express your needs <u>unapologetically</u>.
    - <u>Speak</u> when it matters.
    - Say <u>less</u>.
    - Remove <u>filler</u> words.
    - Never <u>undersell</u>.
    - Cut the <u>excess</u>.
    - When in doubt, fall back on <u>experience</u>.
    - Say "I'm <u>confident</u>."
    - Mind your <u>tone</u>.
- Stand your ground with <u>difficult</u> <u>people</u>.
    - When they insult or offend:
        * Give it a <u>long pause</u>.

- Slowly repeat what they said.
  - Keep breathing out.
- When they belittle, patronize, or condescend:
  - Make them say it again.
  - Ask a question of outcome.
  - Reply with silence.
- When they're rude or dismissive:
  - Give it a short pause.
  - Ask a question of intent.
  - Wait.
- The five types of bad apologies are:
  - The no-empathy apology
  - The no-apology apology
  - The excuse apology
  - The toxic apology
  - The justification apology
- When they interrupt you:
  - Let the other person interrupt you.
  - Use their name.
  - Correct the behavior.
- How to disagree better:
  - Apply the *Is it worth it?* filter.
  - Use your vantage point.

- Establish your boundaries.
    - How to say no:
        * Say no.
        * Show gratitude.
        * Show kindness.
    - How to build a boundary:
        * Define your perimeter.
        * Know your manual.
        * Enforce your boundary.
            1. Begin with the boundary.
            2. Add the consequence.
            3. Follow through.

Rule 3 Review

Rule 3: Say it to connect.

- How to frame a conversation:
    - Set a direction.
    - Call your shot.
    - Get their commitment.
- How to stop your defensiveness:
    - Catch yourself.

- Let their words fall.

- Get curious.

- How to prevent their defensiveness:

    - Instead of *you*, begin with *I*.

    - Don't ask *why*. Instead, ask *what*, *when*, or *how*.

    - Acknowledge them first.
        * Tell them what you agree with.
        * Tell them what you've learned.
        * Tell them that they're helpful.

- How to have difficult conversations:

    - Set aside real, undistracted time.

    - Drop the pleasantries.

    - Begin with your end.

    - Be a safe space.

YOUR NEXT STEPS

You've put in the time. You've put in the work. Throughout these pages, I'm proud of the way you've reflected on your own triggers, learned to regulate your emotions, and prepared for removing the *difficult* from difficult conversations. Enough of worrying about how you could've changed what you said last. You're ready for what to say next.

I can't thank you enough for using this workbook. If you follow me on social media and you're here—hi again, it's still me. Thank you for believing in my work and joining me on this mission for a better world, one conversation at a time.

What about the next steps?

I want you to go to:

thenextconversation.com/newsletter

If you enjoyed *The Next Conversation Workbook* and these exercises, then you'll like my free newsletter in which I share one easy, practical communication tip to jump-start your week. You'll also be the first to know about any new projects and writing, and you'll gain early access to any events where I'll be speaking. If you're looking for a next step, this is the first one to take.

And, if you'd like to take two steps, you're always welcome in my online community. There you'll find a searchable library of my content filled with on-demand videos, downloadable scripts, and live classes. Go to:

thenextconversation.com/member

Also by
Jefferson Fisher